ETIQUETTE GUIDE TO
CHINA

Know the rules that make the difference!

BOYÉ LAFAYETTE DE MENTE
REVISED BY PATRICK WALLACE

TUTTLE Publishing
Tokyo | Rutland, Vermont | Singapore

Contents

Preface. 7
Notes on Pronunciation 9

Part I   **The Middle Kingdom**

Chapter 1   **The Origins of Chinese Etiquette**. 13
               The World According to Lao Tzu 15
               Folk Tales and Proverbs 16
               The Wonder That Was China!. 17
               The Eclipse of the Great Chinese Civilization 18
               The Communist Regime of Mao Zedung 19
               Opting for the Capitalist Road! 21

Chapter 2   **The New China** 26
               China's Little Emperors to the Fore! 28
               China's Female Etiquette Guru. 29
               Chinese Etiquette in the New Global Age 30
               The China Web 33
               Jail, Censorship, and the Great Firewall 36
               Westerners in the Chinese Digital World. 39

Chapter 3   **Cultural Influences on Chinese Etiquette**. 42
               The Yin-yang Principle. 43
               China's Dragon Culture. 44
               The Power of Feng Shui 45
               Lucky Numbers in China 46
               How the Chinese View Foreigners. 47
               Women in Present-day China. 50
               The Role of Face in Chinese Etiquette. 51
               What/How vs. Why/Because 54
               Law vs. Reality 54
               Public Rights vs. Private Rights 56
               Connections vs. Competence 57
               Using the Back Door in China 58
               Hong Kong: China's Old Wild West 59
               China's New Wild West. 61

Part II   **Minding Your Manners in China**

Chapter 4   **Personal Etiquette in China** 65
              Using Family Names. 65
              Using Given Names. 67
              Bow or Shake Hands? 68
              Hand Gestures and Body Language 68
              Watching Your Tongue in China! 69
              The Importance of the Apology 70
              Yes & No in China 71
              Chinese Modesty. 72
              Home Visits. 73
              Dating & Marriage in China 73
              Intimate Behavior in Public 74

Chapter 5   **Chinese Meals and Celebrations** 75
              The World of Chopsticks. 76
              Alcohol in China 77
              Tea–China's National Drink 78
              The Honorable Guest Factor 79
              Tipping as a Symbol of the New China 79
              The Chinese-style Banquet. 80
              Sitting in the Right Place. .81
              Chinese Wedding Banquets. 82
              Celebrating Birthdays in China. 83
              Gift Giving in China 83
              Bamboo Gifts. 86
              China's Jade Culture. 86

Part III   **Doing Business in China**

Chapter 6   **Foreigners and the Chinese Way of**
              Doing Business. 89
              The Changing Role of Foreigners in the
              Workplace 90
              Dealing with 56 Chinas! . , , ...95
              China's Government as Big Brother 96
              The Language Barrier. 99
              The Culture Barrier. 100
              Professional Education & China's Political
              Culture. 102
              The Dossier Factor in Chinese Life 103
              Women in the Business World . . . . . , , ...104

Social Etiquette in Chinese Business 104
To Succeed in Business You Must Have Face 106
The Role of *Guanxi* 107
The Value of Introductions. 108
The Information Black Hole. 109
Using the Back Door in Business Relationships. . . . 109
Don't Rotate Managers 110

Chapter 7   **Cultural Influences Vital in Chinese Business** . . . 111
Business as Guerilla Warfare 111
The Senior/Junior Factor 112
Chinese Business: The New Generation 113
The Secrecy Syndrome 116
Two-Dimensional Thinking vs. Three-
    Dimensional Thinking. 117
Production vs. Consumption. 117
Collective Well-being. 118
Group Orientation vs. Individualism 119
China's Emphasis on Self-sufficiency 121
Personal vs. Group Accountability 121
Open-ended vs. Closed 123
Intellectual Piracy in China 124

Part IV   **Negotiating in China**

Chapter 8   **The Chinese Way of Negotiating** 127
The Power of Face 127
The Friendship Factor. 128
Thinking Holistically 129
Facts & Truth vs. How Things Are Done. 129
Patience Is The Key 130
Never Forget; Never Forgive 131
Ultimatums Are Taboo 132
Technology High on the List 132

Chapter 9   **Preparing to Negotiate in China** 133
Social Status Counts 133
Senior People & Negotiating. 134
Field the First Team 135
Learn How to Use Interpreters. 135
Bring Your Own Interpreters 136
Leave Lawyers Out 136
Pay Attention to Small Details 137

Beware of Using Humor 137
Dress the Part 137

Chapter 10   **What to Expect While Negotiating** 139
The Business Card Imperative 141
Addressing the Senior Person 141
Sit Up Straight & Stand Tall! 142
Keep a Damper on Your Enthusiasm 142
Make a Series of Short Presentations 143
Keep Notes at Meetings 143
Confirm Mutual Understanding & Summarize
    the Meeting 143
Ask the Right Questions 144
Striking Like a Snake 144
Withholding Information 145
The "Hit-Run" Tactic 145
The Passive Face Ploy 145
Silence as a Negotiating Tactic 146
What to Do When They Leave the Room? 146
The Intimidation & Anger Tactics 147
Using Competitors as Bogeymen 148
Compromising the Right Way 148
Authority Levels Matter 149
Using Go-betweens 149
Keep on Negotiating! 150

Chapter 11   **Business Entertainment** 152
Business & Official Banquets 153
Reciprocal Banquet Hosting 154
Alcohol & Business 155
Answering Personal Questions 156
Gift Giving Is Dangerous 156

Chapter 12   **When You Are Host in Your Own Country** 158
Getting Personal 159
Structuring the Meeting Room 159
Providing Refreshments 160
Preliminary Remarks 160
Giving Your Guests Face 160
Inviting Guests Out for the Evening 160
Paying Bills 161
Seeing Your Guests Off 161

Appendix

Selected Vocabulary & Useful Expressions......164
Personal Titles...............................164
Family Relationships.........................164
Corporate Titles.............................165
Government Titles 165
Everyday Expressions........................166
Useful Sentences............................166
   Saying hello and good-bye..................166
   Getting to know each other.................167
   In conversation 168
   At the restaurant 169
   At the office..............................170
   At the hotel 170
   On the road 171
   Technology and communications............172
   Money 172

Helpful Vocabulary..........................174
Glossary of Terms Related to Digital
   Communications 181
Index.......................................186

Preface

Most Westerners think of culture (when they think of it at all) in terms of the arts, literature, and music, but these elements are only a small part of culture. Culture is also the way people think, talk, and behave, as well as the way they work and what they create. The various mental constructs that people have of their own existence, of life in all of its forms, and of the universe at large are products of their cultures. People are programmed by their cultures to view and react to the world in certain ways, and it is this programming that unifies them into individual civilizations.

The traditional culture of China is one of the most enduring and powerful ever to have been developed, and because it is the force that motivates and guides such a large number of people it is one of the world's most important cultures.

Wenhua (wen-wha), the Chinese term for culture, can be translated as "patterns of thought and behavior." The Chinese have traditionally viewed China more as a cultural entity than as a landmass, and in the past some writers have suggested that the country should be called *Zhong Hua* (Johng Whah), or "Middle Cultural Essence," instead of *Zhong Guo* (Johng Gwoh), or "Middle Kingdom."

China's culture is so powerful that Chinese whose families have lived abroad for several generations are often still culturally identifiable as "Chinese."

Throughout most of China's long history, the relationships between people in all classes were based on carefully prescribed forms of behavior that addressed virtually every aspect of conduct. This was true to such a degree that learning and following proper etiquette was one of the major facets of life. And the higher one was on the social ladder, the more meticulous and demanding were the rules of etiquette.

The Chinese word for etiquette, *li* (lee), originally meant "rite" or "ritual", referring to the fact that following officially sanctioned etiquette required detailed knowledge of hundreds of correct forms of behavior.

Training in this highly prescribed way of living was so thorough, so pervasive, that people were judged first, last, and sometimes only by how closely they followed its rules of behavior. Etiquette was equated not only with learning in general, but also with culture, morality, and even nationality and nationalism.

The Chinese eventually came to believe that theirs was the only correct form of etiquette in the universe, and that all who did not follow the same meticulous rules of conduct were uncivilized barbarians. Of course, the rules of etiquette in China today are no longer enforced by harsh feudal sanctions as they once were, and have been considerably relaxed. But they remain very important.

Despite the attempts of Mao Zedung and his communist regime to destroy all vestiges of China's traditional culture, and despite the inroads made by Western cultures since then, most of the core values and basic behavioral patterns that have existed in China for more than two thousand years are still very much in evidence throughout the country. Formalities in business and formal situations are still ingrained in the behavior of the Chinese.

While some of China's common customs are quite different from Western mores, others are similar. But in spite of any similarities, they often differ in ways that can spell success or failure for uninitiated foreigners.

It is therefore extremely valuable for visitors to China to have a working knowledge of the basics of Chinese etiquette, and it is vital for businesspeople, diplomats, and others going to China for professional reasons to know the ins and outs of Chinese thinking and behavior.

Since the last edition of this book, there have been momentous changes within China. By GDP, China is now the second richest nation in the world. The larger Chinese cities now look and feel just like cities in more developed nations, though there are still large pockets of poverty within China, especially in rural areas.

However, most people have access to cell phones, computers, and the Internet. Even if their home lacks a landline, it seems that just about everyone in China has some access to the digital world, giving people a degree of connection with others and access to information and news that would have been unheard of even just a few years ago.

Flush with dollars, Chinese students, tourists, and businessmen have become a common sight in the West. Riding upon this wave of internationalization, the Chinese government has helped finance and push Chinese language learning outside of China as a part of its soft diplomacy program, and more people overseas are learning Chinese than ever before. At the same time, China has dramatically increased defense spending, and has taken on a more robust military posture in Asia, much to the alarm of its neighbors.

In many ways, China has come into its own as a nation. Having said this, there are dark clouds on the horizon. The Chinese economy has finally started to slow, and many people question whether the Chinese government can manage a soft landing. Meanwhile, it appears that the government itself is making internal changes, the outwardly visible manifestation of which is a strong anti-corruption campaign, though there are hints of many more changes below the surface.

Times have become uncertain, and given the uncertainty of the times and China's newfound place in the international community as a business leader and a military power, understanding how to work with the Chinese people has become more important than ever before.

Notes on Pronunciation

What has traditionally been referred to as "the Chinese language" is in fact a family of ten closely related but mutually unintelligible languages that includes Cantonese, Shanghainese, Fukienese, Hokkien, Hakka, Chin Chow, and Mandarin. There are also several dozen regional dialects within these languages that are used by some of the 56 officially recognized ethnic groups in China.

Following the takeover of China by the Chinese Communist Party in 1949 it was decreed that Mandarin, the primary language of the Beijing region, was to be the country's national language. All schools outside this region would teach it as a second language, no matter what their native dialect. As a result of this decree, younger generations of Chinese outside of the Beijing area including Hong Kong–are generally bilingual. Visitors who would like to communicate in Chinese even on a basic level are therefore advised to study Mandarin.

It is worth noting that people in all of China's regions have historically used the same ideograms for writing their various languages. Although pronunciation is unique to each language, the meanings of the characters are the same. This makes it possible for people to communicate with one another, no matter which dialect they may speak.

There are four basic tones in Mandarin: first tone (high-level), second tone (rising), third tone (falling-rising), and fourth tone (falling). While most of the sounds in the language are easy for English speakers to emulate, getting the tones right can be a challenge because many words are spelled and look the same but have different meanings based on how they are pronounced.

Getting the tones right requires a combination of keen hearing, imitation, and practice. This begins with knowing how the vowels and consonants are pronounced. Here is a quick guide to their Romanized versions:

VOWELS

a	as in *ah*
ai	as in b*uy*
ao	as in h*ow*
e	as in f*ur*
ei	as in d*ay*
i	as in s*ee*, or, when following the consonants *c*, *ch*, *r*, *s*, *sh*, *z*, and *zh*, as *ur*
ian	as *yen*
ie	as in h*ere*
iu	as *you*
o	as *a*we
ou	as in h*ow*
u	as in w*oo*
ü	as *urr*
ui	as *way*
uo	as *war*

CONSONANTS

c	as the *ts* in ca*ts* or ra*ts*
h	as in *h*ah or *h*ow
j	as in *j*eans
q	as the *ch* in *ch*eap
r	sounds like a combination of *j* and *r*
x	as the *sh* in *sh*een
z	as the *ds* in fa*ds*
zh	as *juh*

Other consonants are pronounced more or less as they are in English.

Part I

The Middle Kingdom

Chapter 1

The Origins of Chinese Etiquette

Nothing says traditional Chinese ethics and etiquette more clearly or loudly than the name Confucius, the great philosopher-teacher who lived from 551 to 479 BC. In his efforts to provide principles for achieving social and political harmony, Confucius taught that society consisted of a hierarchy of overlapping relationships between people. These relationships were a ruler to his subjects, a father to his son, a husband to his wife, an elder brother to his younger brother, and a friend to a friend. With the exception of friend to friend relationships, all of these relationships involved people of different status.

In the Confucian world, everyone should cultivate *yi* (ee), which means "virtue"; *ren* (ren), which means "benevolence"; and *li* (lee), which means "etiquette". *Li* is packed with a multitude of nuance and meaning that is not found in the English word "etiquette". The Chinese character refers to the making of sacrifices on an altar, in the sense of offering proper respect to another person. From this, we get the idea of "rites" and "rituals". And indeed, in traditional Confucian thinking etiquette has a very strong ritualistic aspect: The way something is done can be even more important than the final result, and the actions of an individual can be even more important than his inward motivations. So long as the proper respect is offered, then one has done his duty.

The way one shows respect is relative to the status of the individual, the kind of relationship, and the situation. For this reason, Confucius found it absurd that there could be any kind of universal law that determined everyone's conduct at all times.

In the natural interplay of human relationships, benevolence flows from a person of higher status to someone of lower status, while respect flows the opposite direction. That is, a ruler should show benevolence to his subjects, and his subject should show him the proper respect. It is therefore a grave impropriety in Confucian thinking to ever challenge or question the motivations or actions of someone with a higher status. Confucius taught that if everyone would merely observe the proper etiquette according to his or her station in life, there would be harmony in the world, and that it is not our place to judge or correct those above us.

When it came to government, Confucius taught that government officials could cultivate virtue by studying ancient Chinese classical literature. In his view, government service should be a meritocracy, with rank bestowed based upon how cultivated a person was. In time, Confucian ideas resulted in the development of a system of imperial examinations, which any man could take. While these exams were supposed to test one's knowledge and understanding of Chinese classical literature, in fact they just tested one's ability to rote memorize long passages of text. A successful candidate would gain immediate employment as a government bureaucrat, with his rank depending upon his test score.

But what if a supreme ruler did not have virtue and did not show benevolence to his subjects? In Confucius's view, a ruler received his divine right to rule via a mandate from Heaven, and this mandate could be withdrawn from an unvirtuous ruler. The signs that the mandate were withdrawn would involve some sort of natural disaster or national calamity. As people did not have the right to question authority, the only time they could rebel against a ruler was if they saw signs that the mandate of Heaven had been withdrawn, and that Heaven had chose someone else to rule.

As the generations passed, Confucius's followers added to, codified, and ritualized the principles he originally prescribed. Because his principles addressed the most fundamental issues in all human relationships and were endorsed and enforced by succeeding imperial courts, they became deeply embedded in Chinese culture.

Over the following millennia the guidelines established by Confucius for proper behavior gradually spread to Korea, Japan, and parts of Southeast Asia, becoming the foundation for the ritualistic etiquette that has since distinguished all of these cultures.

However, in China (as well as in adjoining Korea and nearby Japan) the form and ritualistic aspects of the Confucian rules of etiquette became so pronounced they often overshadowed the original essence and purpose of the prescribed behavior. This had positive as well as negative effects.

On the one hand, profound belief in the Confucian principles and the ritualistic behavior this required served as a bulwark of support for the imperial court and government officials, and contributed enormously to the long survival of Chinese civilization.

On the other hand, the restrictive elements in the Confucian code of ethics that supported this ritualistic etiquette prevented the vast majority of Chinese from being able to think and act as individuals, stifled their ambitions, and greatly limited their options and their horizons.

China's immense size, combined with its civilization that was more advanced than its local neighbors and its early isolation from Western nations, resulted in the Chinese looking upon their country as the center of the known world and their culture as superior to all others. This was to have a profoundly disastrous impact on the future of the country, as it led Chinese leaders to ignore the industrial revolution in Europe and the emergence of Western countries as military powers with aggressive colonial ambitions.

The World According to Lao Tzu

Although Lao Tzu (also known as the Old Master) is not as well known in the outside world as Confucius, he was one of the primary creators of China's traditional culture—and according to some legends was a mentor to Confucius.

According to some scholars, Lao Tzu was born in 604 BC and died in 531 BC. He is credited with having written the *Tao Te Ching* (often translated as "The Way"), one of the most significant treatises in Chinese philosophy. This influential work discussed individual spirituality, interpersonal dynamics, political strategy, and numerous other topics. It expounded on the nature of human beings and the ideal relationships they should have with one another, their government, and with the cosmos at large.

One of his most influential teachings was that one should avoid explicit intentions and proactive initiatives—a prohibition that was to become so embedded in Chinese culture that it is still discernible.

Charles Lee, an authority on traditional and modern Chinese culture and author of the insightful book *Cowboys and Dragons,* writes that the teachings of Lao Tzu were and still are more relevant than those of Confucius. According to Lee, Confucian philosophy was followed by the ruling class while the philosophy taught by Lao Tzu and his successors became the ideology of the common people, among whom they lived.

While Lao Tzu was the founder of philosophical Taoism, there is another form of Taoism that centers on the worship of various gods from ancient Chinese folk religions. The highest of these is the Jade Emperor, who rules in Heaven over a myriad of lesser deities. In religious Taoism, these gods control most aspects of human life, including whom one will marry. As these deities can be at times fickle or capricious, people wanting success or good luck will offer them sacrifices.

Folk Tales And Proverbs

Along with Confucianism and Taoism, many Chinese people have found inspiration and moral instruction from old folk tales and sayings. Some of the folk tales are legends involving various Taoist deities, while some are mythical or even true stories about people from Chinese history. Examples would include the story of Hou Yi, the archer who shot down the nine suns, and his wife Chang'e, who flew to the moon; how Cao Chong weighed an elephant; how Zhuge Liang gathered 100,000 arrows; and how Yugong moved a mountain.

These old stories have often proven to be inspiration for Chinese proverbs, called *chengyu* (chung-yoo). *Chengyu* are written in classical Chinese and follow a strict four-character form. In many cases, they give such a pithy summation of a story's moral that they are relatively meaningless unless one knows the story behind them. It is estimated that there are as many as 5,000 *chengyu* in the Chinese language, and many of these are commonly used in daily life.

As we shall see in the next section, since the 1949 Communist take-over, many of the traditional teachings within China have been de-emphasized or at times even ruthlessly suppressed. However, this has not been the case, by and large, of old folk tales or proverbs. Instead, the government has incorporated these into the education system and has used them as part of the youth's moral education, at times reinterpreting them to suit their political agenda. Indeed, in a famous and often quoted speech, Chairman Mao retold the story of how Yugong moved a mountain to stress the need for perseverance, reinterpreting the story as an allegory of how China would overcome imperialism and feudalism.

Along with these old folk tales, a new folk hero emerged in the 1960s, and has been used to inculcate morality among the youth—Lei Feng. Lei Feng (1940-1962) was an army soldier who died in a traffic accident. Shortly after his death, he became the focus of an intense propaganda campaign within China, as an example of selfless sacrifice for the Chinese people. Photos of Lei Feng surfaced showing him helping others and doing good deeds. A diary also emerged, extolling Chairman Mao, expressing zeal for his country, and revealing his desire to fan the flames of revolution among his brethren. This all belies the real question of whether or not Lei Feng even existed— something even some Chinese scholars doubt.

Nevertheless, Lei Feng is held up as a moral example even now, and Lei Feng Day is celebrated by schoolchildren each year on March 5 with visits to old folk's homes or to the local park to pick up litter.

The Wonder That Was China!

In the centuries following the lives of Confucius and Lao Tzu, China experienced remarkable periods of innovation and invention that would make it the most technologically advanced country in the world.

Randy Smith of Monterey Peninsula College has noted in his writings that one of the greatest secrets of history is the immense contribution ancient China made to world civilization. The list of inventions and discoveries of the early Chinese is astounding, and equally remarkable is that many of their breakthroughs in knowledge and technology did not reach the Western world—or occur there independently—until hundreds or even thousands of years later. For example, Smith notes that "modern" paper was invented in China in AD 105. In contrast, papermaking was not introduced in the West until the eighth century, and the first paper mill in Europe was not built until 1009.

Similarly, an early compass was invented in approximately AD 200 when a Chinese metal smith discovered that magnetized pieces of iron always aligned themselves in a north-south orientation when placed on pieces of wood floating in a bowl of water. This primitive compass was refined over the centuries and the first true compass is said to date from around AD 900. It was not until the fifteenth century that Europeans became aware of magnetism.

Other Chinese discoveries and inventions that better-educated Westerners are generally familiar with include silk, gunpowder, and rockets.

For well over three thousand years China also led the world in the treatment of various diseases and in preventive measures designed to ensure optimum health—some of which, particularly acupuncture and tai chi, are only now finding acceptance in the West.

Smith credits the development of agricultural technology for the extraordinary growth of civilization in China, listing such innovations as row cultivation, intensive hoeing, and the use of the seed drill as major factors. Here China also outpaced the West: the first seed drills did not appear in Europe until the sixteenth century AD, although in China they came into use in about 1500 BC.

The Eclipse of the Great Chinese Civilization

During most of the last millennium of Chinese civilization's heyday, the cultures of European nations were in the throes of what came to be called the Dark Ages—a stagnant period when the fall of Rome and domination by the Christian church resulted in religious faith replacing reason and logic in the affairs of the state and people.

While there was no dark age in China, by the beginning of the fifteenth century the imperial government stopped promoting and rewarding innovation, in effect making it taboo. Emphasis was shifted from looking ahead to looking backward, and from invention and creativity to revering the past and maintaining the status quo. Creativity in China dried up, and its great civilization began a slow, steady decline. For the most part China's creativity was not to flower again until modern times.

From the sixteenth to nineteenth centuries a series of invasions and incursions by newly industrialized Western nations caused upheaval in China, and then in the early 1930s a massive invasion by Japan combined with a communist-led civil war to further devastate the country. Shortly after the end of World War II in 1949 the communist revolutionaries became the masters of China.

The Communist Regime of Mao Zedung

By the time Mao Zedung and his communist forces took over the country in 1949 the ancient wonder that had been China for more than three thousand years had virtually disappeared. The lights that had shone so brightly in the Middle Kingdom had gone out.

During the first decade of his rule Mao actually made many social and economic improvements in China. He gave women the right to vote and reformed the ancient tenant farming system. He established a system of universal education and decreed that Mandarin was to be taught as the national language.

But his attempts to rebuild the industrial infrastructure of the country in "Great Leaps" forward ended in disaster, bringing death and untold suffering to millions. In a final desperate attempt to remake China in his image of a communist utopia in 1966, Mao initiated the so-called "Cultural Revolution," which was intended to eliminate all vestiges of China's traditional culture—specifically the heritages of Confucianism and Taoism. Mao's goal was to totally eradicate these traditions because he understood their weaknesses and did not want communism to mutate into a mixture of the two.

Mao's armies in his new revolution were made up of millions of young people—mostly students—whose lives had been disrupted beyond reason by the results of centuries of war and turmoil. These were the infamous Red Guards who embarked on a ten-year frenzy of burning libraries and destroying temples; intimidating, torturing, and killing members of the educated class; splitting up families; and sending millions of city dwellers into the countryside to force them to live like peasants.

During the chaotic Cultural Revolution, Mao's government condemned refinement in behavior as a ruling-class plot to inhibit people and keep them down. His Red Guard minions went to extremes to destroy China's ancient cultural heritage of etiquette.

Present-day Chinese sociologists blame Mao for the virtual disappearance of good manners during his reign. Historians note that Mao himself was coarse and vulgar and delighted in flouting convention. During the Cultural Revolution being called a *dalacu* (dah-lah-tsu), a "big, rude guy," was a compliment that was pursued in earnest by top leaders.

The Cultural Revolution was motivated by a desire to do away with traditional values and mores, pitting young people against their parents and teachers in a way that would horrify Confucius. However, the Cultural Revolution did not result in an eradication of traditional values within China—they still hold a potent power of many Chinese people, and later government initiates have at times stressed the need for traditional morality.

Indeed, in 1971, the PLA stepped in to gain control over the young members of the Red Guard, sending many of them to work in the fields as peasants, all of the while stressing the Taoist theme that the students should mind their own business, and just tend to their own fields without worrying about what others were doing. As Lao Tzu said,

> There should be a neighboring state within sight, and the voices of the fowls and dogs should be heard all the way from it to us, but I would make the people to old age, even to death, not have any intercourse with it.

This kind of thinking informs the behavior of the generation that came of age during the Cultural Revolution even to this day.

An enduring legacy of Mao's Cultural Revolution was the disappearance of virtually all of the more stylized forms of etiquette that had distinguished the Chinese for millennia. This was compounded by the new market-orientated society, where survival and achievement became more important than ritualized etiquette. It was to be several decades before the importance of good manners was to become a matter of national concern.

Opting for the Capitalist Road!

The Red Guard reign of terror and destruction in China did not end until Mao died in 1976. Mao was followed in power by Deng Xiaoping, an old revolutionary cohort who had been removed from his position in the government and exiled to the countryside after making known his disillusionment with Mao's ideas and methods.

Recalled to Beijing by other members of the politburo who had also become disillusioned, Deng was soon to become famous by declaring, "To get rich is glorious!" It is said that an independent-minded daughter of a high-level general made this comment first; Deng apparently just adopted it.

Deng's epochal new capitalistic ideal was also the result of outside inspiration. He adopted it after a visit to the coastal city of Shenzhen (Shen-jen), where Deng saw that entrepreneurs from nearby Hong Kong had transformed the area into a dynamic manufacturing and shopping center far beyond anything else in China. Beginning in 1978 Deng initiated reforms that were to set the country on the road to capitalistic wealth and power.

The initial benefactors of Deng Xiaoping's reforms were agricultural workers, because the farmers could now bring their crops directly to the market and keep the money they had earned. Another group which benefitted greatly from the reforms were party cadres. With the decentralization of government control over the economy, they had plenty of opportunities to become wealthy by lining their own pockets through corruption and graft. However, reforms occurred much more slowly in the commercial and industrial sectors, to the detriment of city-dwellers and people with university degrees. At the same time, even though society was becoming more open and people had many more opportunities and choices than ever before, the government itself was not keeping pace with social and economic reforms.

This all reached a breaking point, resulting in the Tiananmen Square protests in 1989. While the student protestors wanted to end government corruption and to speed up government reforms, one key factor underlying their discontent was a lack of economic opportunities for themselves.

After the protests were put down in June, 1989, the Chinese government gradually shifted its policies from agricultural reform to privatization, with many government factories and businesses being spun off into private companies which were completely responsible for their own bottom line, even though they were partly or wholly government owned. These state owned enterprises (SOEs) were not bound by the old rules, and could hire or fire whomever they wanted.

With the growth of SOEs, many Chinese people began to groan that "the iron rice bowl was now broken"—that the promise of full employment and a government salary until the day they died was no longer going to be kept. This was only partly true, as the government made great efforts to insure that these SOEs stayed afloat through easy bank loans and favorable treatment. However, with privatization and the loosening of economic restrictions, the private sector experienced rapid growth. This growth intensified after China was admitted into the WTO in 2001.

With this economic growth, people flooded into the big cities looking for high-paying jobs, something the national government has encouraged. In the year 2000, only 36% of the people of China lived in cities, but by 2014 this figure was 53.7%, and the Chinese government plans on raising it to 60% by 2020. Thus, within less than a generation, China has turned from being a largely rural, agrarian society to an urban, industrialized nation, with white-collar wages approaching those found in developed countries. Indeed, in 2011, China surpassed Japan as the world's second largest economy.

Not everyone has shared in this prosperity, however. Rural areas have become an economic backwater as farming income has declined, and in many cities—especially Shanghai, Shenzhen, Guangzhou, and Beijing—new arrivals have often found themselves relegated to low-paying jobs, and barred from receiving public benefits because they cannot get a residence certificate, a *hukou* (hoo-koh).

With economic reforms there has come in increased interest in the rule of law and greater fairness and openness in how the law was applied. This has been especially true in cities such as Shanghai, which effectively have become laboratories to test out policy initiatives before they are rolled out nationwide. While there are sometimes unexpected anomalies in the way the law and various government rules and regulations are understood and enforced in a city like Shanghai, in daily life the legal system there is in many ways just as transparent and above board as in many developed countries.

This is certainly not true throughout China, however, and there is still a great disparity between how the law is administered in the big metropolises, and how it is administered in rural villages and small cities.

This emphasis on rule of law has not extended to the decision-making apparatuses of the central and local governments. If anything, the government is less open, less transparent, and more restrictive of press and individual freedom now than at any time since 1989.

The pressing problem for the Communist Party has been how to maintain control over the country in the face of economic reform and openness. The answer was to take steps to strengthen its control over the government and over the Chinese culture and media, and to increase party membership. In 1989, the party had 47 million members. However, by 2015, the party membership had risen to 87.8 million members—an 86% increase, even though the population had only grown by 21%. Now, instead of complaining about corruption, many of the educated elite could take part in it and share the wealth.

Things came to a head in 2012, with the Bo Xilai incident. Bo Xilai was the party secretary for Chongqing in southwestern China, but he had aspirations to become leader of the country. As noted by Carl Minzner of Fordham Law School,

> Breaking with long-accepted political norms that emphasized low-key public personas for up-and-coming cadres, [Bo Xilai] aggressively cultivated a charismatic populist image during his tenure from 2007 to 2012. His signature tactics included mass rallies, a revival of Maoist "red" culture, and an intense campaign against "organized crime" that swept up criminal suspects, legitimate businessfolk, and their lawyers alike.

However, the world came apart for Bo when his chief of police fled to the US consulate in Chengdu to escape retribution for investigating Bo's wife regarding the murder of a British businessman. The chief of police carried with him an extensive dossier on Bo's activities, and both the chief of police and the dossier fell into the hands of the central government in Beijing. While things become murky at this point, if the stories are to be believed, Bo conspired with the head of state security, Zhou Yongkang, to wiretap the top leaders in the central government in view of gaining leverage to become elevated to the top spot in the government, and possibly even mounting a coup d'état.

Now with Bo's wife, the chief of police, Bo Xilai, and Zhou Yongkang safely in prison, Chinese leader Xi Jinping has effectively adopted many of the same tactics that Bo Xilai used in Chongqing, but on a national scale. Xi Jinping has amassed more personal power within the Chinese government than any man since Deng Xiaoping, and he is now building a personality cult around himself. Further, the government is promoting Maoism on a scale that has not been seen in a generation, as Xi Jinping seeks to center all of Chinese society around the Communist Party. In this regard, there is a government push to insist that all private companies within China should have Communist Party cells operating within them (as this is not yet a law, it appears that foreign companies may be exempt).

Oddly, Confucianism is now being emphasized by the government, as it seeks to gain greater control over society. In particular, the Confucian concept of filial piety is being promoted. Filial piety is the respect someone should show towards his father or ancestors. In this case, however, the Communist Party has reinterpreted filial piety to mean respect for the government and its leaders.

Finally, Xi Jinping has initiated a seemingly never-ending anti-corruption crusade. Thus far, more than 70,000 high-level party officials have been disciplined for corruption. The government claims that this is all in the name of strengthening the rule of law in China. However, there is a real question as to whether this anti-corruption drive represents "rule of law" or "rule by law". In a nutshell, does the law apply equally to everyone in the country, or is Xi Jinping just using the law to weed out possible opposition to his rule?

Now that the Chinese economy has started to show signs of slowing, given all of the fissures within Chinese society—between the urban poor and the urban rich, between cities and rural areas, between those working in private companies and those still working directly for the state or in SOEs, between the communist old guard and those who joined the party for personal advancement, etc.—there is a real question as to where the country is heading in the future.

As Minzner sums up,

Uncertainty hangs in the air. Chinese with the most to lose are diversifying against risk—placing their money in Vancouver real estate and their children in U.S. colleges, and maybe even seeking passports from one or another of the small Caribbean nations that is known to put citizenship up for sale.

The events of 1989 did not resolve the core question of China's political future. Nor did they put it on hold indefinitely. Rather, they launched a cascading set of effects that have swept through China's politics, economy, and society in the years since. The resulting reverberations have now begun to dislodge core elements of the institutional consensus that has governed China for decades. A new future is slouching toward Beijing to be born.

Chapter 2

The New China

History has shown that cultures generally change slowly, except when life-altering new technology is introduced. Such technology can cause cultures, no matter how hidebound, to change virtually overnight. This is now the case in China, a culture rapidly transforming in response to a wholesale introduction of new technology that is changing the way its people think and live.

The new China can be both startling and awe-inspiring to first-time visitors. Signs of affluence and modernization are every-where, particularly in the eastern cities. In that part of China one has to go to the countryside for more traditional sights.

Perhaps the only thing that has remained constant in China is its mass of people. If you haven't had the experience of walking in lock-step to avoid treading on the heels of other pedestrians in shopping and entertainment areas you cannot begin to appreciate what being crowded can mean.

However, in the downtown areas of Shanghai, Beijing, and other Chinese cities it is easy to imagine that you could be in the most upscale shopping areas of Chicago, New York, London, or Paris. The people are well-dressed, many more fashionably so than their foreign counterparts. There are ritzy restaurants as well as familiar fast-food outlets, attractive cafés, and high-end boutiques.

In other words, the externals of much of Chinese civilization in the major urban areas have changed dramatically. (Except for Chinese food, which appears to be eternal.) But what has not changed that much for the vast majority of older Chinese, especially in rural areas, is their internal culture—their etiquette and ethics, the attitudes and behavior that make them Chinese. Despite the modern facade that is spreading throughout China it is this internal traditional culture that attracts—as well as confuses and stresses—many foreign visitors.

Then there are the post–Cultural Revolution urban generations, born after 1976. These generations have had upbringings so different from their parents' that they qualify as "New Chinese." They are more individualistic, independent-minded, and spontaneous in their behavior, all attributes that were taboo before the advent of New China and are very familiar to Americans and other Westerners.

This is particularly true of the new breed of entrepreneurs who have become rich and behave in nontraditional ways, either because they never learned traditional behaviors as children or because they have discarded them.

In spite of the cultural changes that have occurred and are still occurring in China, even the New Chinese still retain many characteristics that set them apart from their Western counterparts. For example the Chinese, like most Asians, are programmed to think of time and events as occurring in a circle, not in the straight line that is characteristic of the thought processes of Westerners. The Chinese cultural encoding to think in this holistic way is far too deep for it to disappear in one or two generations.

Another thing that continues to distinguish all Chinese, especially those who are in the mainstream, is a powerful sense of patriotism and nationalism that pervades virtually every thought and action.

Some perspectives have changed, though. The new breed of Chinese no longer believes the old idea that foreigners should not be allowed to learn anything about China—even as the Chinese made extraordinary efforts to learn everything possible about foreigners—or that foreigners who display an intimate knowledge of China are both dangerous and an embarrassment.

However, China's government continues to control the spread of American-style pop culture into the country by prohibiting much of the vulgarity that is presented as entertainment in the West. In Chinese talent shows, for example, government guidelines allow no vulgar songs, no tears, no outlandish hairstyles or apparel and no mocking or humiliating behavior by the judges. When these restrictions proved to be not strong enough, the Chinese government simply cancelled a slew of new talent shows that were soon to hit the airwaves, and ruled that the current shows could no longer be shown during prime time. How long these restrictions will be enforced is a matter of conjecture, as modern-day Chinese have a history of ignoring government controls they disagree with.

Like much of the rest of the world, China has undergone major social changes since the end of the Cultural Revolution in 1976. Revolutionary advances in technology, from television to the Internet, are only the beginning. For both visitors and businesspeople who hope to make the most of their time in the country it is important to understand the impact of the following cultural influences.

China's Little Emperors to the Fore!

As important as China's one-child-per-couple government policy has been since it was inaugurated by Mao Zedung, there has long been concern that the system would cause its own kind of serious social problems, including a breakdown in traditional Chinese etiquette.

This worry sprang from the tendency of parents with just one child to seriously spoil that child, especially if it was a boy. From the 1980s on, this symptom of the one-child law was clearly discernible among more affluent families, so much so that the children of such families were commonly referred to as little emperors.

This new generation of "un-Chinese-like" children is usually dated from 1978, when the country's new Open Door policies began making it possible for well-off parents to indulge their children with the trappings of capitalism. Most of the children affected were in the educated upper class, and they began moving into positions of leadership early in the twenty-first century.

The fear that the one-child system would water down what remains of China's traditional etiquette has become a reality. Most young people in China are more interested in getting ahead than in conforming to the old ways.

In part because the wealthy have always been able to find a way around the one-child policy, and in part out of fears that China may be entering a demographic crisis with too many old people and not enough workers, in 2013 the Chinese government relaxed the one-child policy, allowing an urban couple to apply for permission to have a second child if either parent was an only child, and a rural couple to apply for permission if their first child was a female. Then, in 2015 the one-child policy was changed to a two-child policy. However, even with the end of the one-child policy, one-child families continue to be the norm.

China's Female Etiquette Guru

Remarkably, one of the most powerful catalysts for cultural change in China since the 1980s has been one person—a woman named Yue-Sai Kan.

As profiled by the _New Yorker_ magazine, Yue-Sai Kan, daughter of famous Chinese painter Wing-Lin Kan, was born in Guilin in 1946 and brought up in Hong Kong. As an aspiring concert pianist, she migrated to Hawaii and eventually went to New York where she found work in the fields of advertising and public relations.

From there she got into cable television, which was still very new to the viewing public, and began helping to produce a program called _Looking East_. The show's popularity amazed everyone, and it ran for twelve years. She also produced the award-winning documentary _China Walls and Bridges_.

In 1984, PBS invited Kan to host a live broadcast from Beijing on the thirty-fifth anniversary of the People's Republic of China. It was so successful that the Chinese government asked her if she would do a television show in China. She accepted the invitation and began producing _One World_. This show made Kan a household name in China and the news media credited her with single-handedly introducing American culture to the Chinese people, as well as exposing the whole world to the complexity and variations of Asian culture.

In the early 1990s, Kan was invited by Chinese friends to become involved in business in China. She chose cosmetics because despite its modern development, she felt China had no color. "The drabness has to go!" she said. "Chinese women should look good and feel good about themselves!"

Kan introduced a cosmetic line in three department stores in 1992. She then wrote a book, _Guide to Asian Beauty_, which became an instant bestseller. Today her Yue-Sai Kan cosmetic line is sold nationwide, and young urban Chinese women are among the most appearance-conscious women in the world.

She then wrote two more books that became runaway bestsellers: _Etiquette for the Modern Chinese_ and _The Chinese Gentleman_.

Kan's _Etiquette for the Modern Chinese_ was aimed at informing Chinese businesspeople, diplomats, and other readers about the ins and outs of Western etiquette, and how to behave toward Westerners and in Western settings. The government got behind the book, ordering copies for its overseas embassies and representatives at the United Nations.

The Chinese Gentleman, which Kan said was sorely needed, is written in Chinese with such English chapter headings as: "How Should a Gentleman Look?" "How Does a Gentleman Eat?" "Gentlemen in Daily Life," and "Ladies and Gentlemen." This last chapter addresses relationship issues from dating to marriage and sex—traditionally taboo subjects in Chinese etiquette.

The book is peppered, at times humorously, with illustrations of gentlemanly do's and don'ts. According to Kan, the book came at a crucial moment in China's development, when Chinese businessmen were coming into greater contact with foreigners without any prior education from parents or teachers about what Westerners considered cultured behavior.

The book, Kan added, was one that men needed and women loved. She added that in traditional Chinese culture, it was always emphasized that men should be well-mannered, well-educated, treat people with courtesy, and think of others. But that this was missing from the present generations.

Chinese Etiquette in the New Global Age

There have long been varying opinions of etiquette in China. China's "perfect" etiquette is spoken of by writers who are not really familiar with the standard of etiquette that actually prevails there, or who are engaged in a kind of soft cover-up. Other sources insist that the Chinese have one of the world's lowest standards of etiquette.

The truth is more complicated than either of these opinions would lead you to believe. There are three facets of etiquette in modern-day China. Firstly, China has traditionally had a very high formal standard of personal etiquette among family, friends, and business associates, and generally speaking this standard still exists. But it is now less ritualistic and rigid than it was in earlier times, and is still evolving, particularly among the internationally minded younger generations.

The second major facet of etiquette in China is the "non-standard" that applies to behavior in public and toward strangers.

This can be described as informal and without set rules. Because of the etiquette demands of the Confucian code of ethics the Chinese have traditionally avoided adding to their social, economic, and political obligations by limiting the requirement for a high standard of behavior until it applies only to family, relations, school friends, co-workers, and guests. This meant that outsiders and strangers in general were more or less nonentities who were ignored. This is the reason why bumping, pushing, and shoving in crowded public situations, without apologies or even acknowledging the presence of others, has long been common in China.

And then there is the third facet of etiquette—or lack thereof—in present-day China that is generally used only by the class of men who spit, urinate, and do other things in public that are offensive to others. This is a phenomenon that has evolved since the decline and fall of the last Chinese dynasty, the many wars, and the breakdown of public order that was epitomized by the Cultural Revolution.

Among the factors that contributed to this situation were the enforced massive movements of millions of people throughout the huge country; inadequate transportation facilities; a lack of public toilets, especially in the countryside; the simple absence of any kind of tissue paper; and finally the growing level of air pollution that made nose and lung congestion endemic.

The downside to China's surge of modernity, however, is the continued existence of industrial pollution in many cities. In Beijing this pollution is often also combined with wind-carried dust from the Gobi Desert. Having to live with this can be an ordeal for anyone. But there is light at the end of this polluted tunnel. Inspired by techniques used in Iceland, the Chinese government has initiated the first steps of a program to tap into the country's extensive resources of geothermal heat. The first test of this project is in the ancient city of Xianyang, which by the year 2000 was one of the most polluted cities in the world. Another positive sign: geothermal pumps were used to heat and cool some of the venues of the 2008 Olympic Games in Beijing.

On many fronts, China's government has come a long way since the days of encouraging rough manners. Since well before its emergence as an economic superpower, the Chinese government has been sponsoring public relations programs designed to curb crude, unsightly, and unsanitary behavior in public, especially spitting and urinating.

As in many other arenas, Shanghai was a leader in this effort. The city came up with what it called the Seven Don'ts—don't spit, don't litter, don't destroy public property, don't damage green areas, don't disobey traffic rules, don't smoke in public places, and don't use impolite language—intending to put an end to behaviors that had long been the rule rather than the exception.

Some government officials have even advocated the elimination of the famous *kaidangku* (kay-dahng-koo), or "open crotch," pants that many Chinese infants and babies are dressed in to simplify trips to the bathroom and potty training—and that foreign news media like to display to the world. (Chinese mothers have been quoted as saying this ancient custom has nothing to do with good manners, and that bureaucrats should mind their own business.)

Around China, urban areas are plastered with billboards calling on people to "act civilized," and not surprisingly it is the younger generations of Chinese, especially the women, who are the most responsible in their public actions, using a style and standard of behavior that combines traditional Chinese elements with Western customs.

The challenge to raise the level of public manners in China remains enormous, however, particularly because of the number of men searching for jobs and on the move throughout the country. Many of them live in the streets and are more concerned about surviving than displaying good manners.

The eating and table manners of people in ordinary restaurants and at food stalls can also inspire serious criticism by both Chinese and foreigners. This has resulted in numerous public and private institutions teaching a common-sense approach to etiquette. Charm schools catering to all ages are now big business in China. Various media outlets even sponsor contests and offer prizes designed to encourage a higher level of public behavior.

Foreign companies operating in China, as well as a growing number of Chinese companies, are now sponsoring programs to teach their employees how to interface successfully with fellow workers, government officials, customers, and the public at large. They see it as an essential element in their corporate culture, with long-term implications for their survival and success.

The China Web

No one can talk about modern China without mentioning the Internet. In the year 2000, only 25 million Chinese people were online, compared to 95 million in the US. However, by 2015, the Chinese netizen population had reached 649 million—nearly double the entire population of the US. The nature of Internet usage has also changed over the years, from young men playing online games in a darkened *wang ba* (wang bah), or net bars, to people of all shapes and sizes accessing the Internet from personal computers in their homes or offices, or increasingly through cell phones via the mobile Internet, in order to make friends or shop.

In its infancy, the only part of the Chinese Internet that was really Chinese were the email addresses that netizens received from their Chinese Internet service provider, which was owned by the government. Chinese netizens generally used Internet Explorer to access the World Wide Web, because that was the default browser on the Windows operating system, and they used Western search engines to find content, because Chinese search engines had not yet been developed. However, since Western companies were slow on the mark in generating products suitable for the Chinese market, in the first decade of the 21st century a host of private Chinese companies began to crop up to meet market demand.

The first of these companies to see large-scale success was Tencent, with its chat platform QQ Tencent (formally known as QQ). Within just a short time after Pony Ma opened his company in 1998, QQ Tencent became a must-have for Chinese Internet users, with many people spending hours a day on it, chatting and playing games. Though QQ Tencent has been surpassed in popularity by other Chinese Internet apps and portals, it is still one of the largest and most popular chat clients in the world. Indeed, it set a world record by having 210,212,085 simultaneous users online in July 2014.

China is an exceedingly large country, which can make it difficult for businesses to reach customers and vice versa. To overcome this obstacle, in 1999 entrepreneur Jack Ma set up Alibaba. In the beginning, Alibaba was just a B2B portal. However, within China there is not a very clear distinction B2B, B2C, and C2C, so when eBay entered the Chinese market by buying the Chinese e-commerce portal EachNet for $150 million in 2003, Jack Ma felt that he had to respond defensively to protect his company. As a result, he started Taobao (ta-oh ba-oh), initially as a C2C marketplace, but later expanding it to offer B2C services as well. Through his drive and his superior understanding of the Chinese market, Ma destroyed his competition, forcing eBay to all but withdraw from the Chinese market in 2006. Essentially, eBay wrote off its entire $150 million investment. Through Taobao and its other merchandising portals, for the fiscal year ending in March 2015, Alibaba had a total gross merchandise volume of $554 billion. Presently, Alibaba sells more goods than Amazon and eBay combined, and the vast majority of this business is solely within China.

It can be difficult for Western companies to compete with Chinese companies when it comes to Chinese-language web-navigation and content, which is why Baidu (by-doo) quickly became China's number 1 search engine after it was established in the year 2000. It currently boasts over 1 billion visits a month.

The Chinese government sees control over the Internet within China as necessary for state security, at times blocking Western websites because it cannot control their content. This has proven to be a boon for some Chinese companies. Arguably, for example, Baidu has profited from Google's problems with the Chinese government, though to be fair Baidu was already a successful company with a large share of the search market before Google's troubles began.

In 2009, however, the Chinese government blocked Facebook and Twitter, because these had become vehicles for spreading news about anti-government riots and demonstrations. A Chinese company, Sina Corporation, jumped into the gap, creating Sina Weibo (sie-nah way-boh), a microblogging platform which combines many of the best attributes of Twitter and Facebook. Sina Weibo quickly became the most popular microblogging platform in China. By 2010, Sina Weibo had won 86.6% of the time China's netizens spent online.

For a long time, the conversations on Sina Weibo were free-spirited and more often than not politically incorrect, and many Chinese netizens depended upon Sina Weibo for news and entertainment. However, under pressure from the government, Sina Weibo began to take steps to gain control over what was posted, and now up to

12% of its content is censored. Increasingly, as well, it began to run advertisements and paid content. The overall effect was to drive away many users, who have migrated to WeChat, which is called Weixin (way-sheen) in Chinese. WeChat is a phone app that was introduced in 2011 by Tencent. It provides chat, text messaging, the ability to broadcast (like Twitter), and the sharing of videos and photos with friends. As of May 2015, WeChat had 549 million active users worldwide (100 million outside of China), and the average Chinese person spent 40 minutes a day on WeChat.

The Chinese Internet is a rough and freewheeling world, full of arguments and discussions between strangers and friends, much like a typical Chinese teahouse must have been 100 years ago. To illustrate the freewheeling nature of the Chinese Internet, one term that has become common in discussion threads is *shafa* (shah-fah), which literally means "sofa". In a typical discussion thread on the Chinese Internet, the first person to comment claims the "sofa", as it is the best and most comfortable seat in the house from which to observe the verbal fracas that will inevitably occur.

Of course, not all of the Chinese Internet is happy-go-lucky. One disturbing trend are human flesh search engines, or *renrou sousuo* (ren-roh soh-suah). This is the Chinese Internet equivalent of a lynch mob. Human flesh search engines feed the need for justice in a country where so often the rich, the powerful, and the well connected can do anything they want without repercussions, even committing murder. The mob sets upon its victim with unmatched fury, putting the victim's address, phone number, private photos, and intimate details on the Internet for all to see as a form of public humiliation. This phenomenon became so marked that famed Chinese director Chen Kaige even made a film about it (*Caught in the Web*). Fortunately, human search flesh engines have become less common in recent years.

What has not become less common are the activities of the 50-cent army, or the *wumao dang* (woo-ma-oh-dang). These are mostly university students working freelance for the government, posing as genuine commentators on Chinese social media, but with the purpose of promoting Communist propaganda, steering debate away from controversial topics, disparaging the US, and inculcating patriotism and love of the Communist Party. According to legend, they are paid *wumao*, or fifty Chinese cents, for every post they make. As it turns out, they are paid considerably less than this, but the name has stuck. No one knows for certain how many paid trolls are in this "army", but it is thought to range in the hundreds of thousands. This is but one of several means that the government uses to try to control online discussion.

Given that there is a 50-cent army which praises the Chinese government, some people suspect that those who disparage the Chinese government are really paid trolls for the Americans. For this reason, people who seem unduly critical of China and worshipful of the US are often accused of being "US-pennies", or *mei-fen* (may-fun), as this must be how much the US government pays them for each post.

Of course, Chinese companies get into the act as well. Many Chinese companies secretly hire people to praise their company on Internet forums, and to run down their competitors. Such people are called a "water army", or *shui jun* (shoo-eh joon).

Jail, Censorship, and the Great Firewall

The Chinese government has made it a national priority to control the Internet within China. It has made anonymous postings on the Internet illegal under Chinese law. In order to set up a blog, join a microblogging platform, open an Internet account, or even access the Internet at a net bar, one has to provide a verified ID, and this ID must correspond to one's identity on the Internet so that one's online activity can be easily tracked. Web sites, portals, apps, and services within China essentially have to lift up their skirts to the government in order to operate legally. The government insists on having their encryption keys, and access to private information about their users upon demand.

While many Western observers supposed that government control over Internet content would become looser over the years, the opposite has proven to be very much the case. The most recent laws governing Internet usage in China mandate stiff penalties, including jail time, for posting content critical of the government or government officials, for disclosing state secrets, and for rumormongering. These categories are all so broadly defined that pretty much any online discussion of the government, government officials, or government policy could be problematic.

While people do go to jail for Internet posts, this usually happens only to those who have a high-public profile, to those who have uncovered some official malfeasance that the government wishes to hide, or to those who are attempting to organize some kind of political activity. People seldom get hauled away merely for venting or blowing off steam.

More typically, the government does its best to censor the content on the Internet. As the Internet is too vast for the government to accomplish this directly, it puts the onus on the various online companies to police the content themselves. The government gives the companies an updated list of topics that should not be discussed on their forums, and confirms that the companies have the proper policies and mechanisms in place to comply with their censorship demands, and reliable party members overseeing the process. If companies do not comply, they are closed down until satisfactory compliance measures are taken.

Many Westerners falsely assume that the government wants to censor negative comment on its policies. This is not quite the case. Rather than merely censoring negative comment, the government typically sets aside general subject areas wherein any content apart from that which has been officially approved by the government is forbidden. It is not that people are not allowed to say something negative about these topics on the Internet — they aren't allowed to say anything at all. And if they try to discuss off-limit topics, the government holds the web platform responsible for shutting the discussion down, deleting the content, banning or suspending offenders, and reporting offenders to the police, if need be.

While many Chinese do not appear to notice or mind government censorship, others display various degrees of irritation with it. Online commentators who stray into dangerous territory are often warned by friends, "Check your water meter", or *cha shui biao* (cha-shoo-eh bie-ah-oh). This phrase apparently came from a popular TV drama, where police gained access to an apartment by claiming to work for building maintenance. The warning means that the police may be at their door.

One common online meme within China is "grass mud horse", or *caonima* (tsah-oh nee-mah). The word refers to an alpaca. However, it is also a pun on an obscene phrase which describes how many

Chinese feel about censorship. Along with "grass mud horse", one is also to find "river crab", or *hexie* (huh-shee-eh). This is a pun on the Chinese word for "harmonious"—it is used to mock the government's censorship efforts, which are ostensibly done to promote a "harmonious society". Of course, all discussion of censorship is automatically censored, so while the Chinese words for "grass mud horse" and "river crab" can often be found on the Chinese Internet, many people just post fanciful pictures of "grass mud horses", alpacas, or river crabs as a form of protest.

All e-companies, including Western companies which wish to operate within China, must abide by Chinese Internet laws. Of course, the Chinese government has no control over the Internet beyond its borders. For this reason, from the very beginning of the Internet in China, the government has tried to block overseas content from entering the country, if that content is viewed as harmful to the state. The result is the Golden Shield Project, which is informally known as "the Great Firewall of China"—the *fanghuo changcheng* (fang-wha chang-chung).

The Great Firewall of China works in several basic ways. If, for example, you are using a search engine and you enter a query that contains any of a number of banned words, the browser page will automatically reset, effectively giving you a time out from using that search engine. This can also occur if you try to access some webpages with banned content, even though the other webpages on a website might still be available. However, in many cases, whole Internet domains and web services are blocked, and you cannot access any of the content they have, even if it is merely to look at cat pictures.

Oddly, it is not illegal to view these webpages or use these web services—no one in China has gone to jail yet for merely using Facebook or Twitter, for example. Nor it is illegal—yet—to try to circumvent the Great Firewall. Thus, from the beginning, people have been playing a cat-and-mouse game with the government as they sought ways around the Great Firewall. The government has responded by strengthening the Great Firewall and plugging up whatever holes it can find. However, this has up to now just proven to be a big nuisance for Internet users rather than an actual barrier.

Of course, the vast majority of Chinese people do not have a strong enough English ability to really manage the Internet in English, and do not have enough of a knowledge of the West or connection with Westerners to really get much benefit from jumping over the Great Firewall. It is true that they would gain access to Facebook, Twitter, and a whole host of other web services. However, there are plenty of good Chinese alternatives for them to choose from. For these reasons, few Chinese really think of the Great Firewall as much of an intrusion into their lives.

There are two things that by and large up until now the Chinese government seems to care little about stopping through censorship or the Great Firewall—pirating and pornography. It is true that every once and awhile some distributor of Internet porn or pirated material gets a little bit too big, and the government takes action. However, for the typical netizen, there seems to be no limitation to finding these things on the Internet within China.

Westerners in the Chinese Digital World

The digital world offers some unique challenges for Western e-companies wanting to operate within China. Western web platforms and services must abide by the same laws as their Chinese competitors. A handful of Western companies have reconciled with this and have at times offered products within China which comply with Chinese law, allowing the Chinese government access to their encryption keys and user data. Other Western companies, notably Yahoo and Google, have for the moment pulled out of the Chinese market altogether rather than comply with Chinese government demands.

China is a huge potential market, so all of the large e-companies would like to enter in. However, in the past Western e-companies have faced strong international repercussions whenever they attempted to comply with Chinese government demands, while at the same time making little headway in reaching Chinese customers. Given the risks, many Western e-companies appear to be taking a wait and see attitude toward the Chinese market.

But what of other foreign companies and foreigners living and working in China? For the individual foreigner living in China, it can be fairly easy to get over the Great Firewall. Meanwhile, it appears that so long as the foreigner is not a reporter, and so long as his activity on the Internet is not in the Chinese language or does not involve heavy interaction with Chinese people, more often than not the Chinese government could care less what he does. However, only a fool would press his luck. Chinese government policy can change without warning, and sometimes the government feels a need to make an example of someone, and foreigners make easy targets.

Foreign companies and businessmen face a very different problem in China, however. For years the US State Department has warned businessmen travelling to China that they should take elaborate steps to protect their digital devices and records from the prying eyes of the Chinese government. While some people scoff at such warnings, knowledgeable insiders suggest that if you have important trade secrets on your work laptop, you should not take it on a trip to China, but bring a fresh, clean laptop that contains only the necessary information for the trip. Laptops, cell phones, and U-disks should always be closely accounted for while you are in China, and you should assume that your Internet activity will be closely monitored. Any company operating within China has to assume that the Chinese government either already has access to all of their digital property, or can gain it quite easily, and so should take suitable countermeasures to keep its data secret if this proprietary information is deemed valuable.

Many international companies have reported problems accessing their overseas servers or the overseas clouds where they keep all of their data and communications. In the past, the way around this was to set up a VPN. However, the Chinese government is cracking down on VPNs, as they are currently the primary way of getting over the Great Firewall. While thus far corporate VPNs have been largely spared, it is by no means certain that this will be true in the future. Any company or businessman wanting to do business in China should consult a reliable tech person to ensure that communications with home can be adequately maintained, and that digital devices, data, and communications can be safeguarded.

At the same time, it appears that the Chinese government may soon be requiring foreign companies to be in complete compliance with their new cybersecurity laws. If this is the case, international companies doing business within China may find using overseas clouds or servers out of the question entirely, and they may have to

hand the government access to the encryption keys to their systems as the price of doing business in China. Everyone is now holding their breaths to see how the new cybersecurity laws will be implemented.

Chapter 3

Cultural Influences on Chinese Etiquette

Confucius still lives in the hearts and minds of most older Chinese, and the social values he taught remain the bedrock of mainstream Chinese society. The family is still the pre-eminent institution in China, and most individuals see their first duty as attending to their family's welfare. Working family members still pool their resources for the economic gain of the entire family.

Within families, courtesy, sincerity, humility, loyalty, respect for parents, and obedience to superiors are still the quintessential essences of Chinese culture. The obligations children have to their core family groups do not end with marriage, and this has been one of the enduring strengths of the Chinese.

Another inherent weakness in Confucian philosophy is evidenced by the "nonstandard" kind of etiquette discussed in the previous chapter; the Confucian emphasis on harmony applies only to one's inner circle of family, relatives, friends, guests, and so on, and not to people outside of it. However, this is one of the traditional cultural factors that is slowly but surely changing in today's China. As people have become individualistic and more independent, they have also come to depend on a wide range of people outside their inner circles— including businesspeople and government officials, as well as other strangers and foreigners.

Naturally, older Chinese people are more likely to still believe in and follow traditional ways, while younger ones are more likely to be modern and trendy in the Western fashion. There are also significant culture gaps between those who live in the interior, rural regions of the country and those who live along the eastern seaboard in the larger cities.

There is no possibility that all of the characteristic mindsets and behaviors that have distinguished the Chinese people for five thousand years will disappear in the foreseeable future. They are reflected in integral parts of the various languages of China, and language is the primary carrier of culture. Furthermore, much of the culture is embedded in the educational system and, in particular, in the government bureaucracy.

But Chinese who were fully programmed in the traditional culture as youths are disappearing at a significant rate each year. Those who came of age during the reign of Mao Zedung (1949–1976) tend to be less traditional than those who came of age earlier. Those who came of age during the 1980s or later tend to be even less traditional with each passing year.

The following sections discuss some of the most important cultural factors that will continue to impact Chinese thinking and behavior for the foreseeable future.

The Yin-yang Principle

It is, I believe, impossible to fully understand Chinese behavior without comprehensive knowledge of the ancient yin-yang concept. The terms *yin* and *yang* are generally known around the world as relating to such opposites as hot-cold, sweet-sour, male-female, and positive-negative. But this understanding of them is incomplete.

The concept of yin and yang is, in fact, an explanation of the nature of the cosmos, the behavior of all organic and inorganic material in the universe, and the invisible energy that infuses the cosmos down to the level of quantum physics. Yin-yang incorporates the creation and extinction of all things in an unending cycle.

Looking just beneath the surface of Chinese behavior reveals that the yin-yang principle applies to relationships between males and females, between seniors and juniors, and between the government and the private sector. In fact, it applies to virtually all relationships and activities.

Chinese scholars and philosophers have been writing about yin and yang since around 1400 BC. Even before this they were acutely aware that yin-yang relationships were not fixed but rather in a constant state of flux, waxing and waning in inverse proportions between hot and cold, strong and weak, and young and old.

Traditional etiquette in China is built around keeping all of these yin-yang relationships in harmony. Having said this, modern China has by and large eschewed many traditional ways of thinking. While modern Chinese might sometimes tend to categorize things in terms of yin and yang, in daily life the need to balance yin and yang is thought of mostly in terms of the food that is eaten and the order in which the dishes are consumed, and China's traditional medical and therapeutic practices. If anything, someone applying the principles of yin-yang might think that modern China is a country very much out of balance, with too much yang and not nearly enough yin.

China's Dragon Culture

China has long had what could be called a dragon culture. Colorful images of Chinese dragons, creatures much more fanciful-looking than Western ones, are common throughout the country.

There are four kinds of dragons in Chinese mythology: celestial dragons that guard the heavens; spiritual dragons that are in charge of the weather, and can cause havoc when fighting or angered; earth dragons that rule the waters and live in seas, lakes, rivers, and ponds; and treasure dragons that are in charge of the precious minerals in the ground.

According to myth a celestial dragon brought the first emperor down from heaven to the Middle Kingdom, and thusly became the badge of the imperial family. The beds emperors slept on were called dragon beds, the ceremonial dresses they wore were known as dragon robes, and the throne they sat on was called the dragon seat.

Mythologically speaking, the ancient Chinese considered themselves children of the celestial dragon. (That's more impressive than claiming monkeys as your relatives!) Dragons came to be the symbol of the nation.

Many of China's celebrations recall the power of dragons, including the Dragon Boat Festival that is held every June. One of China's most festive events, its traditional dragon boats are believed to bless the water they pass through. This gave rise to the tradition of people bathing and washing their hair in the water after the boats have passed, in hopes of having good luck for the rest of the year.

Dragons appear in other Chinese festivals in the form of the dragon dance, which features a team of people carrying a large dragon puppet. This dance has been popular for more than a thousand years.

While the dragon culture of China has little to do with everyday etiquette, it is worth knowing about because of its symbolism in Chinese life.

The Power of Feng Shui

The ancient Chinese phrase *feng shui* (fung-shwee), which literally means "wind and water," refers to the way the power of nature affects all things, including people.

Now part of the world's international vocabulary, the concept of feng shui is not fully understood even by most people who know it and use it.

Dating back some six thousand years, feng shui is a system of divining knowledge about the influence of nature based on a combination of astronomy, astrology, geology, physics, mathematics, philosophy, psychology, and intuition. In the theory of feng shui the universe and everything in it, down to all of the elements that make up the human environment, is composed of energy.

It is believed that this natural cosmic energy—known as *qi* (chee)—has a direct impact on the health, emotions, and welfare of individuals. If you and the things around you are not in harmony with nature, various forms of bad luck and suffering will result.

According to feng shui practitioners, this energy has a positive and a negative flow. If homes, businesses, and other structures are built with their front sides and doorways open to its positive flow people who live or work in them, as well as activities that occur there, will prosper. By the same token, if buildings are not orientated in conformity with the flow of positive energy the results will be negative.

The traditional Chinese belief that every aspect of things desirable in life—good health, a long life, a good marriage, financial security, and so on—was affected by this force of nature is still important.

Although most people today in China are aware of the principles of feng shui, many do not put much stock in it. A few Chinese are very enamored with traditional Chinese thinking, and may arrange their homes or work environments according to the principles of feng shui because they really believe in it. Others do so not out of firm belief, but because they want to hedge their bets. However, most modern mainland Chinese do not show much concern for feng shui, except possibly in business plans and marketing campaigns, not because they believe in it, but because there might be the odd customer or client who does take it into consideration.

It is an important advantage for foreigners in China, especially those doing business there, to be aware of this ancient teaching and its ongoing role in Chinese life. It is wise to make a point of conforming to it, especially when constructing homes or other buildings, arranging furniture, and so on. Businesspeople should, in fact, bring in a feng shui expert to advise them on construction and interior furnishing projects.

One of the remarkable things about feng shui is that an awareness of *qi* and its influence is felt intuitively by many people in most cultures, particularly old cultures in which people still have a close relationship with nature.

Lucky Numbers in China

Like people in other cultures, the Chinese believe some numbers to be lucky and others unlucky. In China even numbers are generally more auspicious than uneven numbers. Some numbers also have special connotations because of their pronunciation.

The number two, *er* (are), suggests germination and harmony. At wedding celebrations, decorations are invariably set out in pairs: a pair of red candles, a pair of pillows, and a pair of couplets hanging on the sides of the hall.

Six, *liu* (leo), conveys its homophonic meaning indirectly: do everything smoothly. Because of this, the number six is commonly used symbolically and is a favorable number for things in general.

Ba (bah), the Chinese word for eight, sounds like *fa* (fah), which refers to making a fortune. Unsurprisingly, eight appears to be the most sought-after number in China.

Four is the exception to the even number rule because this Chinese word for it sounds like *si* (su), which means death. When people choose car license tags, phone numbers, room numbers, and so on, they try to avoid fours and to get as many eights as possible.

Among odd numbers, seven implies anger and abandon, while nine sometimes signifies longevity and eternality.

In China, numbers can also have more explicit meanings. When young lovers send roses, one rose means "you are my only love"; two roses mean "we are the only two in the world"; three roses mean "I love you"; and nine mean "everlasting love."

Lucky numbers can also be important in the Chinese zodiac and feng shui.

One of the most interesting and telling stories about lucky numbers in China involves the Japanese department store chain Yaohan. When the company opened its first store in Beijing a clever manager put a 14–carat gold pen on sale for 88,888 yuan—at the time the equivalent of $11,000. The pen was the first item the store sold when it opened for business. (Contrary to this auspicious beginning, the chain later failed and temporarily withdrew from China!)

How the Chinese View Foreigners

As is well known by history buffs, for more than three thousand years the Chinese looked on all foreigners as uncultured barbarians. Given the appearance and behavior of the vast majority of outsiders they came into contact with over the millennia, this judgment was not that far off—witness the great walls the Chinese built over two thousand years ago in hopes of keeping hostile barbarians at bay.

By Chinese standards the first Westerners to show up in China in significant numbers were indeed uncultured and ill-mannered. Compared to the stylized and ritualized etiquette of the Chinese, the manners of the Western sailors who began arriving during the sixteenth century were sorely lacking; they were often looked upon as louts and ruffians even in their own countries.

During the first of the long centuries of Western activity in China, the vast majority of Chinese who lived in rural areas and in the huge hinterlands never saw a foreigner, and had no source of information about them other than rumors and propaganda. And for a long time after the arrival of Westerners, ordinary Chinese who lived in the cities and coastal areas were forbidden to talk to or associate in any way with foreigners. The stereotype of foreigners being unlettered and dangerous barbarians thus survived in most of China until the early twentieth century.

Despite the huge number of foreign tourists who visit China annually and the growing number of expatriate families who live there, the presence of foreigners in much of the country is still rare. When they do show up in more isolated areas they are generally stared at with wide-eyed curiosity, much as a Texas cowboy might be stared at by a sophisticated New Yorker.

For the most part the curiosity about foreigners that one still finds in remote areas of China is friendly, and the innate hospitality that is an integral part of Chinese culture is readily obvious in the treatment of foreigners once personal contact is made.

Chinese students in particular like nothing better than practicing their English by accosting foreigners, an exchange most Westerners appreciate as much as the Chinese students do. In the past this has led to an uncountable number of friendships that transcended time and place.

Not surprisingly, many Chinese believe stereotypes about foreigners that can be negative. Among the common beliefs are that all foreigners (especially Americans) are wealthy, big and clumsy, have ugly facial features, and know little or nothing about China. Foreign men are often seen as having sexual designs on young Chinese women. There are, of course, flip sides to these stereotypes, including that foreigners, once again Americans in particular, are kind and generous and helpful—and so naive that it is easy to take advantage of them.

On a deeper cultural level, older, more sophisticated Chinese still tend to feel that their five-thousand-year-old civilization and its cultural accomplishments over the ages make them inherently superior to most Americans and Europeans. (To help overcome this perception that their civilizations are cultural and historical newcomers, Westerners can remind Chinese contacts that their cultures are deeply rooted in ancient Greece and Rome, and therefore compare favorably to Chinese civilization in terms of antiquity.)

Mao-era propaganda that the democratic principles of the United States and some European countries were evils intended to destroy China, and that capitalism was a scourge designed to make a few people rich by exploiting the poor, have been left on the dust-heap of history by most Chinese.

Most young Chinese, like most young people in the rest of the world, are intensely attracted to the open cultures of the United States, Canada, Australia, England, and other Western nations. Many are also vitally interested in learning about and visiting Japan, the first Asian country to become an economic superpower by imitating and cooperating with the United States and other Western countries.

The Chinese are more familiar with Americans in general than they are with other Westerners because they have had much more to do with the United States since the 1800s. There is a very old belief that the United States is a "gold mountain," a land of unprecedented wealth and opportunity. That this image is in part a mirage has long been recognized by the Chinese, but enough of its power remained that until the first decade of the twenty-first century the greatest ambition of many Chinese was to study, work, and live in the United States. By the beginning of the twenty-first century, though, the incredible economic boom in China had resulted in more and more Chinese who were overseas returning home and fewer of the best and brightest opting to leave the country.

While in earlier times the Chinese referred to Westerners as barbarians, they are now formally called *waibin* (wie-bean), which means "foreign guest" or "foreign friend." Informally, they are also called *lao wai* (lough wie), which literally means "old foreigner," but the connotation is more like "old friend."

Since the policy of reform and opening up was initiated in the early 1980s, China has in general welcomed foreigners with open arms and has often given them a rather privileged place in society as people who are helping China develop. However, attitudes towards foreigners are changing and becoming more nuanced. While few Chinese people are openly hostile to westerners and Chinese people will generally try to offer foreigners good hospitality as guests, there is a growing sense that foreign expertise and money are no longer as needed, and that foreigners do not deserve a prominent place of honor and respect. Indeed, some Chinese may even feel that foreigners need to be put in their place. This is especially true in the large cities, but not so much in rural areas which are still struggling to develop.

Women in Present-day China

The Chinese constitution and other laws provide equal rights for men and women in all spheres of life, including ownership of property, inheritance, and educational opportunities. (A marriage law that gave women property and inheritance rights was in fact among the first laws adopted after the founding of the People's Republic of China in 1949.) But nonetheless the women of China have not been fully emancipated from many constricting traditions of the past.

According to Human Rights Watch/Asia, equality between the sexes has been a part of the agenda of the Chinese Communist Party (CCP) from its early days, but women's rights are perceived to be in a separate category from human rights. When women's rights or interests conflict with Party or government policy, the latter takes precedence.

Abuses related to the government's family planning policy are not reported in the media or discussed publicly. Information about other issues, such as the extent of domestic violence, trafficking in women, or abuses directed at lesbians, is effectively stifled by the CCP's injunction that most news must be positive. Thus, the controls on freedom of expression and association have a strong impact on women's human rights.

Most of China's provinces, autonomous regions, and municipalities have local laws against domestic violence. Laws were passed in 1980, 1992, and in 2007 to further prevent discrimination against women in employment and education, but they are generally not enforced. Indeed, the income gap between men and women has widened in China within the past 30 years, and gender discrimination in employment has become increasingly the norm within China, even though it is explicitly against the law. There is a law mandating compulsory primary education, but large numbers of both boys and girls in rural areas are not sent to school because their parents think the cost is a waste. It is now estimated that some 30 million people in China are illiterate—and 70 percent of them are female.

During the first decade of the 21st century, there was a growth of NGOs and public activism within China, in many cases promoting the rights of women. However, recently the Chinese government has begun to reign in most NGOs and nearly all public activism. For example, in 2015, five female activist were arrested by the government because they had planned to raise awareness of the problem of sexual harassment on public transportation. While the Chinese people are in many ways more outspoken than ever before in asserting their individual rights, the government holds that the collective rights of the Chinese people must override any individual concerns, and so it views public activism as harmful to the state, even if the purpose of the activism is to help people become more aware of existing laws and official policies.

Women now make up a sizable percentage of China's workforce, and hundreds of thousands of them are college graduates engaged in professional occupations ranging from engineering and medicine to business administration. Some 42 percent of China's civil servants are women. However, only 23 percent of party cadres are women, and a woman is half as likely as a man to become the chief official in a government department, an SOE, or a public institution.

Large numbers of Chinese women, many of them educated in both China and abroad, are also employed in managerial positions by international companies. Some foreign companies in China employ as many or more women as men in their front offices. Women are especially prominent in the hospitality and tourism industries.

The Role of Face in Chinese Etiquette

The cultural factor that plays the most significant role in Chinese etiquette in both social and business situations is subsumed under the word *mianzi* (me-in-zu), which may be translated as "face," "personal honor," "an acute respect for oneself," and in many circumstances "having a very thin skin."

Until the last few decades of the twentieth century it was difficult or impossible for ordinary Chinese to develop a strong sense of self-esteem because the culture in which they lived denied them the right to think and act independently and prevented them from being able to demonstrate their own individual worth or take credit for personal accomplishments. Failure to abide by the ancient taboos against these things—many of which were codified as law by the imperial dynasties and continued by the Communist regime—was regarded as immoral and unethical by traditional standards and could have serious consequences.

However, there were two key ways that individuals could stand out quietly and unobtrusively. The most important of them was to develop, to an extraordinary degree, skill in an art, craft, or other endeavor—and that is exactly what many Chinese did over the generations.

Having *mianzi* was the other way that the Chinese were able to feel good about themselves without breaking any taboos. Unblemished reputations for living up to all the cultural expectations that built up over the centuries were vital.

In fact, having face was historically more important than having some kind of special expertise. Economic and social survival depended on the former because any serious blemishes on one's reputation would prevent one from making and keeping the kind of *guanxi* (gwahn-she), or "connections," that were essential for survival in an authoritarian society.

Now, for the first time in their history, private Chinese are mostly free to pursue individual goals, to take pride in their accomplishments, and to otherwise act as individuals. But the importance of having social connections and face have hardly diminished. Both concepts are so deeply embedded in the culture that they continue to play leading roles in the everyday lives of the people.

Today there are many aspects of *mianzi* in Chinese culture. They include the status of your family, the school you attended, your financial situation, your appearance, your intelligence, your expertise or lack thereof, and whom you know.

In Western cultures many of these factors are more or less fixed and the power or strength of one's face generally remains intact, but this is not the case in China. In China your *mianzi* is as changeable as the weather. And to the Chinese, it is an internal as well as external thing—your image of yourself as well as the image others have of you.

The Chinese are culturally programmed to refine and define things down to their smallest units, and *mianzi* is no exception: It is broken down into four basic categories.

Although the order in which these categories are ranked seems arbitrary, *liu-mian-zi* (leo-me-in-zu) is especially key because it refers to the vital importance of the good reputation that one gets by avoiding mistakes and making what turn out to be wise decisions.

In my judgment the next most important category of face is *gei-mian-zi* (gay-me-enn-jee), which is made up of any action one takes to give face to others by showing them respect or paying them compliments.

Another category of face is *jiang-mian-zi* (jahng-me-in-zu). This refers to your own face being increased by the actions of others who treat you with respect or say complimentary things about you to other people. This is often the best kind of face to have.

The final category of face is *diu-mian-zi* (dew-me-in-zu). It refers to actions or events that are embarrassing or could represent a setback or a danger to you and become known to other people, resulting in you losing face.

These categories generally apply only to relationships with those in your inner circle, rather than everyone you meet. Nonetheless, each category is critically important to achieving any kind of success in China. It is especially important to avoid losing face or causing others to lose face. The latter can cause a lot of problems because it demands some kind of reciprocal action.

The surest way to cause someone to lose face is to insult them or criticize them in front of others. Westerners might also offend Chinese unintentionally by making fun of them in the good-natured way that is common among friends in the West. It is also possible to cause someone to lose face by treating him or her as a junior when his or her official status in an organization is high. People should always be treated with the level of respect that is proper for their status according to Chinese standards. Failure to observe this cultural requirement can result in both the offender and the mistreated party losing face among those aware of the situation.

As indicated above, just as face can be lost, it can be given by praising someone for good work in front of peers or superiors or by thanking someone for doing a good job. Giving someone face earns their respect and loyalty, and it should be done whenever the situation warrants.

Naturally, it is not a good idea to overpraise others because the obvious insincerity will result in you losing face.

In addition to giving others face, you can save their face by helping them avoid embarrassing situations. A face-saving and face-giving technique that is well known in the West, where it is often used on golf courses, is deliberately letting an opponent win in order to make him or her look good.

In short, one of the primary keys to getting along in China is to avoid embarrassing anybody or making others angry with complaints, criticisms, or other forms of behavior that are upsetting by local standards.

What/How vs. Why/Because

Chinese culture focuses on what/how, while Western culture focuses on why/because. The Chinese (and all other Confucian-oriented Asians) are more interested in the "what" and the "how" of human behavior than they are in the "why." Westerners are more interested in the "why."

Americans in particular are constantly asking "Why?" in ordinary conversations as well as in debates, and they tend to approach presentations in why/because ways. This is difficult for the Chinese to deal with because they believe it to be adversarial. In the context of Chinese culture, the why/because way of thinking and behaving was settled a long time ago, so the Chinese no longer have to think in those terms.

The best way for Westerners in China to overcome this cultural barrier is to present issues in the context of "if we do things this way we will get this result," or "by doing it this way..." and so on.

Law vs. Reality

Well over two thousand years ago both Confucius and Lao Tzu taught that the more laws a country has the less law-abiding its citizens will be. The subsequent imperial governments took their warnings to heart and passed very few laws, generally not even publishing those they did pass.

Confucius and Lao Tzu believed that people's intuition and common sense would tell them when something was wrong, and so they wouldn't do it. And according to these philosophers, if there was any doubt about whether a law existed people would shy away because they knew that if they behaved wrongly in the eyes of their families and the government their punishment could be swift and final, regardless of whether there was a law against their actions.

Chinese attitudes toward the law have not changed that much in modern times. While the laws of China are now published and can be easily found in libraries or on the Internet, they can be vague and open to multiple interpretations, and so it is often difficult to know how the laws will be enforced—or even if they will be enforced at all—until you see them in practice.

In most cases in the past, the laws tended to be only selectively enforced. The Chinese motto "Kill the rooster to scare the monkey" has been used so often to describe the way the law has been applied in China that it has become a cliché. However, it is nevertheless apt, as the general trend has always been to make a high-profile example of some unfortunate soul in order to scare everyone else, rather than to enforce the laws equally and across the board.

This attitude is slowly changing, however. While many laws are still broken with impunity by just about everyone in the nation, some laws, particularly involving matters in daily life, private companies, and government corruption, are seeing more uniform enforcement than ever before, although some people still appear to be above the law.

On all levels of government—national, regional, provincial, and city—laws are passed and enforced only to the benefit that particular entity. As a result many provinces and cities have laws that apply only in their areas, without any federal oversight, though there is a growing trend to make the laws more uniform throughout the country.

With this new emphasis on rule of law, some Western companies have found themselves with a big target on their backs when it comes to law enforcement, as the Chinese government looks for another rooster to kill, or as Chinese companies seek to use the law to rid themselves of foreign competitors. A Chinese judge is unlikely to view with sympathy the defense that someone broke the law because everyone else was doing it. For this reason, in this new climate it behooves western companies to obey the law rigorously in China, even if it might put them at a competitive disadvantage. It is imperative that foreign companies planning to go into China research the laws in the cities and provinces where they want to do business.

Public Rights vs. Private Rights

Generally speaking, the Western principles of democracy and the rights of man are based on legally protected private rights—the rights of individuals to think and do as they please as long as their behavior is not harmful to others. In China, on the other hand, legally protected private rights did not exist until recent times.

The Chinese constitution guarantees the freedoms of religion, speech, and the press, along with the right to assemble. In 2004, the constitution was amended to include a guarantee of human rights and the right to property. Copies of the constitution can be found in nearly any bookstore in China, and you will often see people browsing through it. However, according to the government, all of the guarantees of individual rights in the constitution fall subservient to the collective rights of the people, as defined by the Communist Party. This creates a strong tension within Chinese society.

Many Chinese young people, no doubt because of government propaganda, honestly believe that their country is the freest, most open, and most democratic country on earth. And indeed, compared to previous generations, they enjoy unparalleled freedoms, and have used this freedom to cultivate a degree of individualism and self-expression that would have been unheard of before 1979.

However, this freedom is much more limited than they imagine. Many older people, especially in the party and the government, hold old-fashioned views and see personal freedom, along with the individualism and self-expression that come with it, as vulgar, uncivilized, and a threat to public order. So long as the exercise of individualism and self-expression flies below the radar of this old guard or no one gets their toes stepped on, it is likely that it will go unnoticed and unremarked upon. On the other hand, if it is noticed, then it is common for the offenders to get a stern phone call from someone in authority over their lives, to be "asked" to the police station "to have some tea" so that they can be informally admonished to behave, or to even go to jail. Given restrictions on press freedoms within China, many Chinese people are completely unaware of how often this occurs, and find themselves in a state of shock when they are called on the carpet for minor transgressions or for activities which would be quite normal in most countries.

While Chinese society as whole is still trying to reconcile public and private rights, when it comes to employment most Chinese workers freely exercise their individual rights, even if it is to the detriment of their employer. In previous generations, many Chinese workers tended to think of the collective good of the people in their work group or institution first and foremost, as there was little or no social mobility. The only way to find an individual benefit in such a circumstance was to work for the benefit of the group, as everyone would more or less equally share in the same rewards or punishments.

This kind of thinking is now almost unseen in China, especially in the big cities and on the eastern seaboard. The new generation of Chinese workers tend to put themselves first, working strictly for the pay and benefits, and with varying concern for the well-being of their company. Many will quickly quit a job if they do not feel that it is offering them enough in the way of personal rewards. Many Chinese will find jobs purely for personal advancement. For example, they will accept a job offer at a foreign firm so that they can get overseas training or education, and then leave their company for a better position at the first possible opportunity. Finding and keeping good staff has become a big headache for many foreign firms in China. A handful of foreign firms have even pulled out of the Chinese market altogether because the employee turnover rate is so high.

Connections vs. Competence

In Chinese society *guanxi* (gwahn-she), or personal connections, is described as an "emotional bank account" or "social credits" that you can draw on when you need any kind of assistance or help.

In both a specific and a general sense *guanxi* is typically more important in China than competence. It takes *guanxi* to get into better schools, companies, and government agencies. As a result, those who have the strongest connections usually get the best of everything, a factor that has a dampening effect on the economy, the government, and the whole of Chinese society.

This situation is one of the reasons why really bright, competent Chinese who do not have the right personal or family connections seek jobs with international firms, where brains and ambition beat *guanxi*.

Despite recognition of the failings of the *guanxi* system it is too deeply entrenched in Chinese society for its use and importance to diminish significantly in the foreseeable future.

Foreigners in China quickly become aware that they must build up a *guanxi* network in order to get things done—even everyday things that are supposed to be done by people with responsibility for them. This is especially the case for foreign businesspeople, but it can and often does impact travelers as well.

Using the Back Door in China

There are many special code words in Chinese culture, and one of the most important of them is *hou men* (hoh men), meaning "back door." When the Chinese want to get something done, whether it involves a government office or a private business, they almost always try to find a back door to getting what they want.

Hou men can refer to a personal connection with someone who works in the appropriate business or government office and can either get things done informally or speed up their formal process. It can also refer to someone with a helpful personal connection who can act as a go-between, using his or her *guanxi* to cause the necessary action.

This is another element of Chinese culture that came about because of a disconnect between people in one's circle of family, relatives, and friends, and outside individuals and government entities.

When it comes to private businesses and SOEs, many building guards typically will not even let a visitor through the front door unless they have been warned in advance that the visitor is coming and has an appointment. And, many lower level employees may be absolutely unwilling or unable to help visitors in any way even if they have an appointment. For these reasons, finding a back door to a company may be essential to business success.

On the other hand, in this new era of rule of law, it pays to tread quite carefully when it comes to back doors to government offices. There was a time, for example, when if you had trouble getting a visa, a back-door connection combined with the payment of an added visa "fee" would certainly do the trick. However, beginning in Shanghai, the visa system has slowly been revamped. Now, in many places in China, the system is completely transparent and above board: If your paperwork is in order and you qualify, you automatically get the visa. The visa officer has little or no discretion on the matter, and if there is a back door it is well hidden and few people can find it. This trend has become the norm for the way many rules and regulations are enforced within China, depending upon the locale and the situation. In many cases, government officials may not have as much personal discretion as before, and any attempt to go around them via a back door may be futile or even counterproductive.

There is strong and widely recognized link between *guanxi*, back doors, and corruption. Given the government's anti-corruption drive, while it may be useful and sometimes necessary to find a back door to a government department or agency in order to get more information or to reach someone capable or willing to make a decision, great caution is the rule of the day. For example, if a government official demands an extra payment to see something through, it is always good to insist upon getting an official receipt from the government department for the full amount of the payment. What the government official does with the money after you leave will be his business— meanwhile you will be legally covered, as the receipt proves that the money paid was not a bribe to the official, but as a discretionary fee to the government department. (This is also true of dealings with the police.) Many businessman have discovered that if they demand an official receipt, the need for an extra payment suddenly disappears.

Hong Kong: China's Old Wild West

Hong Kong has always been one of the world's most exciting places to live and do business, and now that it is a prime gateway to the rest of China it is even more attractive.

Locals say the most distinctive feature of the Hong Kong business environment is the interplay between new entrepreneurial-type firms and old, conservative managerial-type firms. Consultants describe the Hong Kong business environment as rampant with entrepreneurship because low taxes and the promise of huge rewards encourage people to start their own companies. There are nearly half a million privately owned small and medium-sized enterprises in this tiny enclave, all of which have the "trader mentality" that goes back to the first days of the former British colony.

Since Hong Kong was returned to China in 1997 the number of big-name multinational companies in the territory has grown steadily. They develop local operations and use the territory as a hub for regional business, a phenomenon that has driven up the demand there for higher education and professional qualifications.

To meet this demand, all these multinational firms have initiated American-style management training programs, dramatically increasing the number of professionals in the territory.

But the flood of new entrepreneurial enterprises has not changed the traditional Chinese approach to business. Virtually all businesses are founded by Chinese families and remain under their control, with decision-making highly concentrated in the hands of the senior member of the founding family.

As these companies grow they bring in technical staff and professional managers from the outside, but the founding families almost always maintain full ownership and decision-making authority. This enables their enterprises to make quick decisions and fast turnarounds as the markets change, giving them an advantage over managerial-type companies.

This typical Chinese approach to business is one of the key reasons why so many enterprises in Hong Kong, on the mainland, and in Taiwan were able to grow so rapidly and why an increasing number of them are becoming major multinational firms.

At the same time, Hong Kong is changing. While it is still a freewheeling business center, since 1997 Hong Kong has become increasingly oriented towards business with mainland China, which has effectively become its economic lifeline. This has resulted in increased corruption and increased mainland control over Hong Kong businesses and politics. Both sides are chaffing under this arrangement. Hong Kongers regularly accuse mainlanders of being uncouth, unsophisticated, and corrupt, while mainlanders accuse Hong Kongers of being uppity, arrogant, and prejudiced.

With the difficulty of finding and keeping qualified staff in China, many multinationals are using Hong Kong managers to take up the slack in their Guangzhou, Shenzhen, Shanghai, and Beijing offices, but with mixed results, as the cultural divide between Hong Kongers and mainlanders is much greater than many outsiders might expect. While the two groups may look the same and speak the same language (many Hong Kong managers have learned Mandarin Chinese), they have experienced divergent histories, and as a consequence have a very different outlook on the world. This can cause interesting personal dynamics when it comes to business, and even some friction.

China's New Wild West

The entrepreneurial spirit of overseas Chinese and Hong Kong Chinese began to appear in mainland China as soon as the infamous and disastrous Cultural Revolution ended in 1976. It developed there slowly, however, because a whole generation of young people had been denied an education and a large percentage of the business class had been stripped of their companies, exiled to the countryside, sent to prison farms and factories, or simply killed off.

After the first conspicuous signs of China's emergence as an economic powerhouse occurred in the vicinity of Hong Kong, more and more Hong Kong–based manufacturers moved all or part of their operations to the mainland.

For many years, it looked like Shanghai had replaced Hong Kong as the new wild west. After all, Shanghai is now the largest city in the country and the third largest in the world. Widely regarded to be the citadel of China's modern economy, it also serves as one of the nation's most important cultural, commercial, financial, industrial, and communication centers. By 2005 it had also become one of the world's busiest ports, and the largest cargo port in the world. Administratively, Shanghai is a municipality of the People's Republic of China that has province-level status.

The city of Shanghai is no stranger to prominence. Originally a sleepy fishing town, it became China's most important city by 1900 and was the center of popular culture, intellectual discourse, and political intrigue during the short-lived Republic of China in the early 1900s. In the late 1800s and early 1900s Shanghai was the third largest financial center in the world, ranking after only London and New York City, and the largest commercial city in the Far East. But after the communist takeover in 1949, it languished under heavy central government taxation and many of its supposedly bourgeois elements were purged.

It was not until 1992 that the central government in Beijing authorized the market-economic redevelopment of Shanghai. The city quickly surpassed early-starters Shenzhen and Guangzhou, and has since led China's economic growth. Shanghai's skyscrapers and modern lifestyle mark the pinnacle of China's economic development.

Yet, while Shanghai has become one of the world's great cities, this focus on Shanghai obscures some truths. First, Shanghai is no longer the only major business center within China. Shanghai still leads the pack, but Beijing, Guangzhou, Shenzhen, and Tianjin have all surpassed Hong Kong in GDP, and Suzhou and Chongqing are not far behind. What was once a business web centered on Shanghai has become a vast network of finance and commerce with multiple hubs throughout the country. Foreign firms which focus only on Shanghai are missing the big picture of what is going on in China, and are ignoring a huge potential market.

Second, the business atmosphere within China has matured. At one time, an international company with deep pockets could simply open an office in Shanghai, and find plenty of eager Chinese companies willing to partner with it and very little competition. It was really up to the company as to whether it succeeded or failed, though it could be said that many failed because they did not do their homework.

Things are quite different now. Foreign firms face stiff domestic competition and increasing hurdles in reaching the Chinese market. While it might appear that there are myriads of Chinese companies wanting to do business with them, many of these firms are no more than storefronts, and it can be difficult at times to sift out those who are worthwhile from those who have nothing good to bring to the table. The need for due diligence is thus greater than ever before.

Part II

Minding Your Manners in China

Chapter 4

Personal Etiquette in China

A Chinese term and cultural concept that foreigners visiting China should know is *keqi* (kuh-chee). The ideogram for *ke* means "guest" and the one for *qi* means "behavior." Together, the compound word means being considerate, polite, well mannered, humble, and modest. Traditionally, these were the characteristics expected of the Chinese, and most of them lived up to expectations. *Keqi* is still the ideal of Chinese etiquette, and generally speaking sums up the kind of behavior that is expected from foreigners.

The word *keqi* most frequently comes up in day-to-day speech as part of the phrase *bu yao keqi* (boo yow kuh-chee), which is understood to mean "you are welcome" but literally translates as "don't be so polite (to me)."

Using Family Names

The proper use of names in China is very important because a respect for them is deeply rooted in Chinese culture. Because of the importance that has been attached to the family unit in China for more than five thousand years, and because families traditionally kept track of their ancestors for many generations, family names took on a semi sacred quality, especially among the upper classes.

The Chinese approach to names is far more formal than in America, for example, and like some European cultures makes significant use of titles.

The general custom is for adults to address each other by their family names, with the appropriate Mr, Mrs, or Miss prefix. In business and formal situations it is customary to attach an individual's title to his or her last name. If Mr, Mrs, or Miss Cho is a manager, for example, the proper form of address is *Cho Jingli* (Choh Jeeng-lee), or Manager Cho.

The formal and official way of writing Chinese names is to place the family name first and the given names last. However, a growing number of people have begun to reverse this order and write their names in the Western fashion. This is particularly true among Shanghai businesspeople who carry on correspondence with foreigners. Another common convention in written correspondence is to print the family name in all capital letters.

The importance of family names in China led to women keeping their family names after marriage. Children generally inherit their father's family name. This too, can cause confusion among foreigners who are not familiar with the custom.

Another element in the etiquette of using family names is that the total number of names available has been more or less limited to those of China's original founding families. This is in contrast to Europe, where cultures were much less cohesive, people's histories were shorter, and where people historically took or were given names based on the work the did, where they lived, and so on.

In China there are, in fact, only about one thousand different family names, and according to the Chinese Academy of Sciences only one hundred of these names are shared by around 85 percent of the Chinese people!

As rendered in Mandarin, the most common Chinese names in descending order by popularity are Wang, Li, Zhang, Liu, Chen, Yang, Huang, Chao, Chou, Wu, Hsu, Sun, Chu, Ma, Hu, Kuo, Lin, Ho, Kao, and Liang. (The next three are Cheng, Lo, and Sung.)

About 93 million people share the name Wang; approximately 92 million are named Li. Some 87 million share the name Zhang.

In 2007 the Chinese government began the process of preparing people for a new law that would allow parents to give their newborns "double surnames" to help reduce the confusion caused by so many single-character names that look exactly alike and are pronounced exactly the same. These names will be written with two Kanji characters instead of the traditional single character, and could be read as Zhou, Zhu, Zhouzhu, or Zhuzhou, for example.

Using Given Names

Among adults in China given names and nicknames are normally used only by family members and close friends. It is common, however, for adults to address children and young boys and girls by their first names when they are introduced.

It is impolite to call someone by only their last name. It is also impolite to call someone by their given name or nickname before you know them well or are asked by them to use it. In the international community, a growing number of Chinese go by the initials of their two given names, like KC, to make it easier for foreigners to remember and use their first names.

This brings up another element in the naming business and use of names in China. Since ancient times virtually all Chinese have had two given names—one selected from the names of their illustrious ancestors, and the other chosen to represent characteristics parents hoped would accrue to their child. When the characters of these names are transcribed in Roman letters, they can be written separately as two names, separated by a hyphen, or—more recently—written together as if they are one name or word.

Nowadays, more and more Chinese families who have become westernized give their children only one given name, eliminating what is often a problem for foreigners.

Because there are so few family names in the country it has long been customary to be very inventive and flowery in the choice of given names, and the Chinese pay a lot of attention to naming their children. Choosing auspicious names for babies is also a serious business because the Chinese traditionally believed that their choice not only determined the child's fate and future, but also affected the happiness of the entire family!

Unlike the United States and other countries, there are no fixed lists of first names in China. Parents have the whole Chinese language to choose from, and the challenge is to pick words that have positive connotations.

Throughout the history of China girls have been given names referring to traditionally feminine virtues, such as beauty (*měi*) and obedience (*xiào*). Boys were named to imply other virtues, such as strong (*gāng*) and wise (*zhì*). Flowers were also popular as female names, while boys could be tigers or dragons.

In the early years of the communist era children were given names such as East Wind, Red Guards, Protect the Nation, and Loves the Party. By the 1980s this political fever had ended.

Diminutives of names are also commonly used in China, as are nicknames. The latter are frequently given by school friends and refer to some characteristic of the individual.

Bow or Shake Hands?

Shaking hands has become a standard custom in mainstream China, among Chinese and also when Chinese are interfacing with foreigners. There are exceptions to this rule in the hinterlands, particularly when elderly people are concerned. When you meet or acknowledge someone who is quite elderly, especially if he or she is seated and not within easy reach, a slight bow is often the greeting.

In formal gatherings involving groups of people when shaking hands is not practical, bowing as a form of greeting is still a common practice. But it is fair to say that shaking hands has replaced the traditional Chinese way of greeting one another.

Hand Gestures and Body Language

In China body language in the form of hand gestures, touching, and the amount of personal space expected is different enough from what is typical in most Western countries that visitors need to be aware of the differences to follow local customs.

The ideal comfort zone between people in China is smaller than in the United States, for example. Perhaps because of the number of people and a lack concern for privacy and keeping one's distance, the Chinese are accustomed to personal space requirements ranging from around one to three feet less than those of Americans.

But while Americans, Latinos, and other Westerners are conditioned to engage in various forms of touching—including hugging, arm-holding, back-slapping, and so on, often with people they may have just met—this is not part of the Chinese experience and can be upsetting. In China such physical intimacy is restricted to family members, relatives, and close friends.

Naturally enough, the growing number of Chinese who have become westernized in their behavior are not as sensitive to these cultural customs, particularly in the travel industry and international business communities.

Various Western hand gestures, however, are still not widely used in China. The Chinese (and other Asians) typically do not point with a single finger, which is considered to be rude. Instead they use the whole hand in a gesturing movement.

The American way of using the index finger to beckon someone is also seen as rude. In this case the whole hand is also used, but not in the typical Western fashion with the palm facing up, fingers curling in, and the hand moving as if pulling the person toward you. Instead, hold your open hand slightly in front of your body, palm down, and move it up and down as if in the traditional Western gesture for good-bye.

Of course, you should use this gesture only to summon people such as store clerks, restaurant or bar staff, workmen, cruising taxi drivers, family members, friends, lower ranking employees, and policemen on the streets. It should not be used when dealing with anyone else, especially government officials or strangers with whom you do not have an obvious customer, guest, or other kind of relationship.

It is also important for visitors to keep in mind that the Chinese smile when they are embarrassed by something—an action, comment, question, or event. This cultural response can be easy for Westerners to misunderstand.

Watching Your Tongue in China!

Foreigners in China are advised to be wary of making comments that could be interpreted as—or are—offensive to the central government. Generally speaking, it is wise to refrain from making any statements that could be construed as critical of the policies of the government regarding the political system of the People's Republic of China (PRC) itself, human rights, and the statuses of Taiwan, Tibet, and Xinjiang.

Another sensitive topic is religion. In the early years of the PRC, religious belief and practice were often discouraged because the government regarded them as backward and superstitious, and because communist leaders like Lenin and Mao had been critical of religious institutions. During the Cultural Revolution, religion was condemned as feudalistic, and thousands of religious buildings were looted and destroyed. However, after the Cultural Revolution's end in 1976 the official attitude toward religion changed significantly. In 1978 the constitution was amended to guarantee religious freedom—with the usual restrictions. Only five religions were recognized by the state: Buddhism, Taoism, Islam, Catholic Christianity, and Protestant Christianity. The government also decreed that belief in any religion was incompatible with membership in the Communist Party, meaning that government employees could not participate in any religious activities or profess to believe in any religion.

Most people in China are not members of an organized religion, but may believe and engage in folk customs and celebrations such as ancestor veneration and feng shui. Millions of Chinese also have informal ties with local temples and unofficial "house churches." Since the mid-1990s there has been a massive program to rebuild Buddhist and Taoist temples that were destroyed in the Cultural Revolution.

Christian missionaries in China—some of whom are in the country undercover, so to speak, as members of aid agencies of one kind or another—are invariably advised to be extremely careful about what they say and where they say it.

Safe topics of discussion include the weather, family matters, children, favorable comments about Chinese food and Chinese arts and crafts, sightseeing attractions, sports, and other such neutral subjects.

The Chinese do not consider it impolite to ask foreigners specific questions about their income. This is a topic of abiding interest to many Chinese, and one that has in the past caused some friction among Chinese employees who were paid much less than foreign co-workers doing work similar to their own.

The Importance of the Apology

Apologies are an important element in all societies, but they are especially important in Confucian- and Taoist-oriented cultures such as China. There social etiquette, not law, is the primary guardian of human rights and people are extraordinarily sensitive to insults, slights, and other things that cause embarrassment or thwart what they regard to be legitimate expectations and activities. This causes the Chinese to apologize in situations that the typical Westerner would ignore, as well as in more serious situations.

Traditionally, an apology was the only recourse the Chinese had in the case of failures in etiquette and worse kinds of behavior. More direct action could bring them to the attention of the authorities, in which case both sides in an argument or conflict could be considered guilty and punished.

Apologies in China therefore carry greater weight than they do in Western cultures. In many common cases, a contrite apology is enough to set things right. Refusing to apologize when an apology is expected, however, can result in serious consequences. In cases involving the authorities this has traditionally meant torture of various kinds, including extreme ones.

Foreigners who inadvertently break a law in China are invariably better off if they apologize quickly and contritely. It is commonly the wisest course of action to apologize even when you are not guilty of anything.

Yes & No in China

The Chinese way of expressing the affirmative and negative might seem to be a small part of China's culture, but is, in fact, one of the most important elements in both Chinese social and business behavior.

The Chinese word for "yes" is *dui* (doo-ce), while "no" is the negation of "yes"—*bu dui* (boo-doo-ee). However, *dui* is rarely used, and *bu dui* is almost never heard. Instead, most people use *yŏu* (yoh) meaning "have", and *meiyŏu* (may-yoh) meaning "not have"; or *shi* (shu) meaning "is", or *bu shi* (boo shu) meaning "is not", depending upon the need. These words can be used by themselves as replies without grammatical subjects.

Traditionally, blunt responses were considered impolite. But even more important is that throughout China's history speaking in such clear, unequivocal terms could be dangerous. Instead people spoke in vague terms or circumlocutions to avoid firm commitments to one side or the other.

The degree of frankness displayed in China can vary greatly depending upon region and social class. Most Chinese people are amazingly forthright, so much so that any ambiguity in conversation can best be understood as an attempt to deceive. Yet, more educated Chinese people might view such frankness as a sign of a lack of sophistication, or even as rude and graceless. At the same time, many Chinese people tend to respond to requests with "yes," even if they are uncertain that they can actually fulfill the requests. This may be done to avoid disappointing or inconveniencing anyone.

By the same token, *maybe* is often the equivalent of no. A response of "no" is also implied when a Chinese person responds to a request with a pained expression on his or her face and says it will be difficult to fulfill. This response is also designed to avoid directly disappointing anyone.

When asked for a favor, most Chinese won't respond negatively in an attempt to avoid embarrassment or loss of face. If a request cannot be met, the Chinese person may say it is difficult, inconvenient, or under consideration, which almost always mean no.

There are numerous occasions, however, when it is important to get an unequivocal yes or no, particularly in business. In these cases it is often necessary to be creative in framing a question in a variety of ways until the real answer becomes clear. There are still numerous occasions when this indirect approach will fail, and it is necessary to bring in a mutually trusted third party to discover the Chinese position.

Chinese Modesty

When it comes to being complimented, the culturally imbued modesty of most older Chinese is still quite strong. They appreciate compliments as much as anyone else, but etiquette calls for them to downplay praise by saying they don't deserve it.

A variety of expressions for downplaying compliments have become ritualized over the centuries, and most people use them automatically whether or not they actually feel modest. For example, it is typical of the Chinese to feign modesty when complimented or praised by saying *"Nali? Nali?"* ("Nah-lee? Nah-lee?"), which literally means, "Where? Where?" and implies "Where is the person you are talking about?" In spite of this behavior, visitors should continue to pay compliments when they believe the laudatory remarks are deserved.

Of course, if compliments aren't truly deserved, or are repeated too often or said in very flowery terms, they will be taken as insincere sycophancy. Both sides will lose face and the compliment will do more harm than good.

Home Visits

The Chinese generally do not invite foreign visitors to their homes. On the rare occasion this does happen, it usually involves people who are fairly affluent, have Western-style homes or apartments, and have had substantial experience abroad. The Chinese typically do their entertaining of guests at restaurants.

If you are invited to a private home, it is customary to bring one or more gifts. If there are children, for example, it pays to know their gender and age and take something appropriate for each of them.

Dating & Marriage in China

Prior to 1949 when Mao Zedung and his communist cohorts took over China, women and men too, in most cases—were not allowed to choose their own spouses. However, throughout history romantic love was common among those in the upper class and, on a much smaller scale, among commoners. For most people this did not lead to marriage.

Mao was determined to break the hold that Confucian traditions like this one had on China, and so quickly passed decrees giving women the right to vote and have a say in choosing husbands. However, until the last decades of the twentieth century marriages continued to be arranged on the bases of class and the needs of the prospective husband's family.

There were a series of steps in these marriages: The man's parents sought out a potential wife for their son; a matchmaker was retained to act as a liaison between their family and that of the potential wife; the respective birthdays were checked to see if they were astrologically compatible; the matchmaker presented betrothal gifts and a betrothal letter to the potential bride's family; wedding gifts were presented; an auspicious day was selected for the wedding; and the ceremony took place.

This kind of arranged marriage and love-matches are both now common in China. In more traditional families most of the old customs are still followed. In westernized families, courtships are Western-style and the marriage arrangements and ceremonies are generally a mixture of Chinese and Western cultures.

Today in China there is also a growing tolerance for interracial dating and marriage. Mixed couples have become relatively common, and are no longer officially or unofficially regarded as undesirable.

Intimate Behavior in Public

Older Chinese are still inclined to regard cuddling and kissing in public as indecent and immoral, but the traditional taboos against publicly displaying affection have gone by the wayside among the younger set in most areas of China, particularly in the cities.

Foreigners in China should not take this westernized behavior of young Chinese as a license to ignore the sentiments of older and more conservative people. The rough and rowdy public behavior that is common in Western countries enforces the stereotype that Westerners in general are uncultured.

Chapter 5

Chinese Meals and Celebrations

Dining in China naturally has its own culturally derived etiquette, but the reality is that foreigners in China do not need to be overly concerned about making mistakes that would upset their hosts or dismay restaurant workers.

The Chinese do not expect visitors to conduct themselves the way the Chinese do, and they are exceptionally tolerant of foreigners who do not know where they should sit in accordance with Chinese etiquette, how to use chopsticks, or the Chinese way of doing anything related to eating and drinking in either formal or informal situations.

Furthermore, the Chinese are typically delighted to guide, instruct, and otherwise help visitors learn enough about their dining etiquette—on the spot—for them to avoid embarrassing mistakes and enjoy themselves. To begin with, you can always depend on your hosts to tell you where to sit.

That said, there are guidelines and insights that should help you make the dining experience in China more enjoyable, as well as give you face.

One important tip is that foreign hosts who have not learned the yin-yang, sweet-sour approach to traditional dining in China should not attempt to order on his or her own. Ordering dishes that do not complement one another and having them served in the wrong order would be something of a culinary disaster as far as the Chinese are concerned.

Learning how to order Chinese food is by itself an interesting lesson in Chinese philosophy. The Chinese are strong believers in the medicinal value of food—not only what is eaten but the order in which it is eaten. Both must conform to the ancient principle of yin-yang—negative, cold, and wet in relation to positive, hot, and dry—to ensure harmony with the needs of the body and remaining in sync with the cosmos. According to this philosophy, sweet and sour tastes should be mixed, a sour dish shouldn't be followed with another sour dish, two sweet dishes shouldn't be served in a row, and so on.

Ordering properly is a very effective way to demonstrate your interest in Chinese culture and your respect for Chinese traditions—both of which will get you a lot of social and business mileage in your dealings with Chinese. If you are hosting a meal, don't know how to order Chinese dishes, and don't have time to learn, get help from a Chinese person.

Visitors to China generally encounter many dishes they have never seen before and may be reluctant to eat, often featuring ingredients they cannot identify. In the past it was common for hosts at smaller banquets to expect foreign guests to try every dish—in part, perhaps, to add to their culinary experience, but more likely to prove that they respect Chinese culture enough to eat what the Chinese eat and have the courage to try new things. This is no longer a hard-and-fast expectation, and you can now choose not to eat a dish without causing an international relations problem. It is wise, however, to say with a smile, "Thank you, but no thank you."

You can expect to see rice at most meals, but in Chinese settings it is not normally served as a main dish at the beginning of the meal; instead it is served as one of the last dishes. However, some restaurants catering to foreign visitors have taken to serving rice with the main dishes.

Some relatively minor actions are considered a bit impolite or thoughtless in China, including taking the last bit of food from a serving platter or bowl, eating every last bite of food on your plate, laying your chopsticks flat on the table, and picking your teeth with your fingers or with a toothpick without covering the process with your hand.

Chinese diners in run-of-the-mill restaurants have long had the reputation of being messy eaters, soiling table covers and dropping bones here and there—something that is often mentioned in guidebooks. But this custom is not common in places frequented by visitors and foreign residents.

The World of Chopsticks

The word *chopstick* is said to have originated in the 1800s among foreign traders who heard Chinese boatmen calling their cooking utensils *kuaizi*, meaning "something fast." The foreign traders translated *kuaizi* into pidgin English as chop-chop, which also came to connote speed.

In China chopsticks have been more than simple cooking and eating tools; over the past four to five thousand years they've also played far more significant roles. During the Tang Dynasty (AD 618–907) chopsticks were made out of silver and gold for the rich, especially emperors. It was also widely believed that silver chopsticks could detect any poisons in food—a belief that was proven to be erroneous a number of times by unlucky diners. According to Chinese tradition, using chopsticks can improve your memory and manual dexterity and is good training for those who want to become painters. In earlier times, left-handed people were required to use their right hands when eating with chopsticks.

In China chopsticks are still used to eat virtually every dish, except soup (eaten with a porcelain spoon), Peking Duck (eaten with the hands), and sometimes desserts (eaten with the hands or with a spoon).

Most chopsticks used in better Chinese restaurants today are made of plastic. They are longer and heavier than Japanese chopsticks. Disposable chopsticks made of wood are gradually being phased out because of serious environmental concerns.

Diners do not grasp these long Chinese chopsticks at or near the top, as foreigners are wont to do. They are held about one-third of the way down, leaving their top ends clean. When using your own chopsticks to serve yourself from a common dish do not use the eating ends of the sticks. The clean top ends should be used for this purpose.

Although some of it is gradually going by the wayside, there is a fair amount of etiquette involved with the use of chopsticks, most of which is very similar to the etiquette for the use of knives, forks, and spoons. It is bad manners to attract attention by beating on the side of a bowl with your chopsticks (something beggars used to do). In addition, dropping your chopsticks is believed to cause bad luck. Poking your chopsticks into a bowl of rice and leaving them upright is a no-no because it is associated with death.

Alcohol in China

Where alcoholic drinks are concerned in China, the traditional custom was to drink before starting to eat but not during the meal. Nowadays, drinking may continue for a while after eating begins. This practice is often encouraged in business or formal situations by underlings in the ranking order who go from diner to diner, refilling cups or glasses and insisting that diners take a drink after each refill.

The traditional drink at such gatherings is *baijiu* (by-jee-oh), which literally means "white liquor". Usually made from millet or sorghum, *baijiu* is an acquired taste for most foreigners, and even some Chinese do not really like it. More westernized banquets may provide wine, beer, or even whiskey as an alternative. However, traditional hosts see the ability to drink *baijiu* as a sign of maturity and masculinity, and so they may insist that you at least try a glass of *baijiu* once before the banquet is finished. At state banquets, Moutai (moh-tai) is famously the brand of choice for *baijiu*, though it seems that every city and province has its own favored local varieties.

The Chinese word for "cheers!" is *ganbei* (gan-bay), which means "dry cup", and can be translated "bottom's up!" Often when this term is used, it means nothing more than "cheers!" and it is possible to just take a sip. However, there are occasions when it is a true *"ganbei"*, and if you do not drain the glass in one gulp the host will be offended.

Refusing to drink in these circumstances can be a serious slight to the host, all of his party, and sometimes to China as well. If you cannot or do not drink it is wise to let your host know in advance. The best excuse is that you have a medical condition and have been ordered by your doctor not to drink. Saying you do not drink on religious grounds does not make sense to the Chinese.

In the big cities, many companies are more westernized, and so it may not be much of a problem to refuse alcohol, and you may even see Chinese people drinking water or soda at a banquet. This is certainly not true in most rural areas, however.

The best tactic to avoid overdrinking when someone keeps refilling your cup or glass is to take just a tiny sip each time. In any event, trying to match the Chinese drink-for-drink is almost always a losing proposition.

Tea–China's National Drink

Tea-drinking began in China several thousand years ago, and tea continues to be the national drink. Home guests are invariably offered tea soon after they arrive. In most restaurants tea is served automatically, just as water is in many American restaurants.

The three most common types of tea served in China are black teas that are fully fermented, green teas that are not fermented, and jasmine tea, which is made of green tea leaves scented with flowers. The tea automatically served in most restaurants is a semifermented green tea called oolong or wulong tea. Eight treasure tea is also popular; it contains chunks of dried fruit and may be further sweetened with sugar. Other so-called "tea" drinks are made from roasted barley rather than leaves of the tea plant.

The etiquette for drinking tea in China is really not that different from elsewhere. Attentive hosts provide refills. In restaurants when the teapot is empty and you want more tea, raise the lid of the pot and leave it up. (This works better in Hong Kong than in some other places!)

The Honorable Guest Factor

There are many positive aspects to China's traditional culture and etiquette, and one of these is the compulsion for treating guests in a hospitable and often grandiose manner. The Chinese typically shower guests with hospitality, as much if not more so than any other people.

Their favorite form of hospitality is to treat guests to meals—often sumptuous ones—in restaurants. "Eating is heaven!" is an ancient Chinese saying, and the Chinese like nothing better than to fully experience this dictum.

On occasions when you extend the invitation to dine out and are clearly the host, many Chinese will still make a strenuous effort to get and pay the bill. The clever and diplomatic way around this (because they gain face and you lose face if it happens) is to slip away from the table minutes before the meal ends and pay the bill in advance—or as some really astute Chinese themselves do, have the money delivered to the restaurant before you and your guests arrive.

Tipping as a Symbol of the New China

One of the signs of the changing Chinese culture is the growing acceptance of tipping service people, particularly in the transportation and hospitality industries. The practice has not yet spread among China's hundreds of thousands of lower-end restaurants, but upscale restaurants, especially those in first-class international hotels and those primarily patronized by the affluent, picked up on the Japanese and Western practice of adding 10 to 20 percent gratuities to their bills years ago.

The Chinese-style Banquet

In my book *China's Cultural Code Words* I proclaim the *yanhui* (yahn-whee), or Chinese-style banquet, to be one of the greatest food orgies available to humankind, designed to please the eye, the mouth, and the mind.

The standard *yanhui* round-table seats twelve people. The Chinese regard this as the maximum number of diners that should be seated at a single table in order to maintain all-around convenience for serving, helping oneself to food, and holding conversations.

As most travelers already know, Chinese meals at home and in better restaurants do not come in individual portions when groups are concerned. They are served on large communal platters or bowls that are set in the middle of the table. The host will usually order one dish per person, which means that a full course meal might consist of one or two cold appetizers, eight to ten entrée dishes and one or two desserts.

In many banquet situations the courses will have been ordered in advance. If not, the hosts at more formal banquets will generally order for the entire group. When a banquet is attended by family members, friends, or co-workers, it is common for the host to take requests from the group.

At social, business, or political banquets that are formal it is very important for the host to personally welcome the guests and see them off when the banquet ends. The host typically makes a short welcome speech and calls for a toast, and the senior guest is expected to respond in kind. If guests at important affairs are not bilingual the host should make sure that one or more interpreters are on hand to facilitate mingling and lighthearted conversation.

If you are the guest of honor at a formal but relatively small dinner party your host may insist on serving you when the first dish arrives—and sometimes from additional dishes as well, depending on how important you are. If there is more than one honored guest the host may start the meal by serving each of them. On such occasions you should accept this form of hospitality gracefully.

Hosts do not always serve guests, however, as the custom varies. Hosts of formal dinners staged for political bigwigs or dignitaries generally do not do any serving themselves, for example. On those occasions this chore is handled by a cadre of waiters.

If you are a guest at a dinner party, do not start to eat or drink before the host does. In a private home, especially one belonging to older or less westernized Chinese, you should not begin to eat or drink until your host has insisted that you do so two or three times.

The Chinese are perhaps even more observant hosts than most Westerners, and make a point of keeping their guests' cups and glasses full and being otherwise attentive to their needs. But none of China's dining and drinking customs are extraordinary or demand any special study or practice. The same etiquette common in the rest of the world is generally sufficient to get you by.

It is polite anywhere to ask guests if they would like more to eat or drink. If you don't want more, just politely decline each time an offer of more food or drink is made. In China hosts may refill the cups and glasses of their guests without asking them if they want more. In such instances, you can wave them off. If they don't take this as a no, you can turn your glass or cup upside down to politely get the message across.

A significant difference between Chinese *yanhui* and similar gatherings in the West is that the Chinese do not drag out the ending of a dinner party. The practice is for everyone to leave immediately after finishing the last course, rather than breaking up into small groups and lingering for private chats. In formal business and political banquets, a final toast may signal the end of the party.

Sitting in the Right Place

There is a precise seating protocol in Chinese dining, both in homes and in public places. Senior members of families and guests get the places of honor in homes, and ranking guests get the seats of honor in public places.

In a formal or semiformal situation in a banquet room or upscale restaurant, your host may direct you to a specific seat that relates to your status. Don't sit down quickly without giving him or her a chance to direct you. In a private home, your host will definitely tell you where to sit.

Chinese Wedding Banquets

The ultimate banquet experience in China has to be the wedding banquet, which is known for extravagance even when staged by people who are not wealthy. This feast is the most important part of the Chinese wedding day, and is viewed to be the true wedding.

Chinese meals are rich in symbolism. Different dishes relate to the happiness, longevity, and fertility of the couple. The number of courses is also significant, because the Chinese are highly sensitive to numbers. Eight is the luckiest number in China, so eight main courses, not including desserts, are traditionally served at wedding banquets.

Among the primary dishes served are fish, roast-suckling pig, chicken, lobster, and a dessert bun stuffed with lotus seeds. These dishes have symbolic as well as culinary value. The pronunciation of *fish* in Chinese is the same as *abundance*, implying that the newlyweds will be blessed with wealth. Roast suckling pig, usually served whole, is a traditional symbol of the bride's purity. Chicken, which symbolizes the mythical phoenix bird, is cooked in red oil to symbolize the wish for a prosperous life for the couple. Lobster is literally called "dragon shrimp" in Chinese. Lobster and chicken served together at a wedding banquet suggests that the dragon and the phoenix—the perfect couple according to feng shui—are harmonious.

At weddings an emcee usually hosts the program and entertains the guests in between courses, while the wedding party takes turns playing tricks on the couple. The highlight of the banquet is when the newlyweds, along with their immediate families, go around the restaurant and make a toast with every guest. The path of this toasting promenade can start from the left or right side of the guest tables, but once started the couple and their families do not turn back on the path they have chosen because that would be a symbol of back luck.

In addition to the traditional Western wedding gifts, couples at Chinese weddings are presented with small red envelopes containing money. The couple collects these packets from the guests as they visit the various tables, or guests can deposit them in a designated box.

Celebrating Birthdays in China

Traditionally the Chinese did not make a big to-do about birthdays until someone reached the age of 60. In the past so few people lived to that age that it came to be a major milestone calling for an all-out celebration.

One of the reasons why celebrating actual birthdays did not develop in China was that traditionally the Chinese believed an infant to be one year old when it was born, and two years old on the first day of the following New Year. This meant that everyone in China automatically became one year older on New Year's Day.

Many in the younger generations have picked up on the Western custom of celebrating birthdays on the actual day of one's birth, when the usual gifts and parties are in order. Birthday cakes bought from a Western-style bakery are typical at such parties, but in a reverse of the Western custom, the person with the birthday is often expected to cut and serve the birthday cake to the guests.

Gift Giving in China

Gift giving has long been an important part of Chinese culture. In addition to gifts exchanged by people personally and privately, it became the custom millennia ago for people to give gifts to government officials to gain favorable treatment. This custom was more or less officially sanctioned on the highest level because most officials in the country were underpaid, and some were not paid at all. Not surprisingly, of course, this custom led to rampant abuse on virtually every level of society, creating a culture of corruption that was to plague the country to the present day.

In the late 2010's, western luxury brands became preferred gifts for government officials. However, the practice of corruption became so bad that the government eventually passed laws making it illegal to give gifts and meted out serious punishment for violations.

Current Chinese law forbids the bribery of both public officials and corporate managers. By Chinese law, bribery entails the giving of gifts with the expectation of receiving some sort of benefit. However, the Chinese government appears to interpret the law to mean that all but very small gifts are in fact bribes, regardless of the intention or whether a benefit is ever received. Expensive banquets, and wining and dining are also covered by the bribery statute. Penalties can include fines, the confiscation of property, prison sentences, and even death. Government officials and party cadres on all levels have been affected by these laws, with the government targeting any ostentatious signs of wealth. This has resulted in the near complete collapse of the luxury goods market within China.

At the same time, it is questionable as to whether these new regulations have really stamped out the bribery of public officials, or have merely made public officials more creative in finding new ways of receiving graft. Certainly, even if bribery is still the norm, in this new climate any foreigner who engages in gift-giving is treading into dangerous waters. So, while it may be necessary to give gifts in China to build personal relations, it is best that these gifts have great personal significance or interest, but very low intrinsic value.

Despite official sanctions against gift giving that verges on or constitutes bribery, the custom of gift giving remains important in China because it is an effective way of creating and building *guanxi*, the connections that are the foundation of virtually all social, business, and political relationships in the country.

Given the historical role of gift giving in China there is naturally some well-established protocol involved. Foreigners probably hear most often that it is good manners to decline a gift at least two or three times before finally accepting it (the same protocol that applies to accepting tea and other refreshments). This especially applies when the relationship between the individuals concerned is new and not yet very close. While this age-old custom generally continues among older Chinese whose mindset and ways are still traditional, a growing number of people are adopting the less rigid Western custom of readily accepting gifts and refreshments.

Some other traditions of gift giving and receiving also exist in China: People who receive gifts feel obliged to give a gift or do some kind of favor in return. The Chinese generally do not open gifts as soon as they receive them, considering this impolite (but you can insist until they relent and do open them). Gifts should not be wrapped in white paper, which is symbolic of death; instead choose red or gold. White things in general usually aren't given as gifts because of their ancient association with death. Clocks and sharp things are on the no-no list because they, too, have negative implications. Don't write thank you notes or other correspondence in red ink because its implications are also negative.

Nowadays, gift giving in China is very similar to gift giving in the Western world. People give things they know the recipient needs or will like, from clothing, jewelry, and special food items to toys for the younger set. It seems that the only old custom that still prevails is that multiple units of the same thing are given in even numbers—other than four, which is associated with death.

This said, in many parts of China it is acceptable to give things in units of five, as this number is associated with the semisacred elements of feng shui—earth, fire, metal, water, and wind.

When giving gifts in China it is, of course, only common sense to choose things that are appropriate for the people involved. Generally speaking, foreign-made items with recognizable brand names may be appreciated. Locally famous products can also be a good choice, especially if they are to be given to families or connections outside of the business world. Foreigners are generally cautioned not to give items that are too expensive or too showy to ordinary people.

You also shouldn't give staple food items because doing so implies the recipient is hungry. In addition, don't give a green hat or cap to a man because that implies his wife is having an affair.

Things that are invariably appropriate for business contacts and others you know on a professional level include cigarettes (if the individual smokes), cognac, well-known brands of whisky, and wines. Nowadays, there are also numerous high-tech gadgets that are often even more welcome than these old standbys.

Again, common sense should be applied in selecting gifts. If you are visiting someone's home an attractive fruit basket or an assortment of popular candies or cookies is almost always appropriate.

One of the safest bets for Westerners visiting China is to travel with a collection of the most popular products made where they live to give individuals who help them in any special way or whom they want to impress and or build a relationship with. This is the very thing that the Chinese themselves, as well as the Japanese and Koreans, do when they travel abroad. These items can be relatively inexpensive if they are just minor thank-you gestures, and of course should be small and light enough to fit in your baggage. In my own case, I take Arizona's famous bola ties for men and small pieces of turquoise jewelry for women.

Bamboo Gifts

Because it is regarded to be lucky in China, bamboo is often recommended by feng shui masters for your home or office. It is also often given as a gift at the start of a new business, the purchase of a home, or simply as a wish for the future prosperity for the recipient. Bamboo symbolizes advancement of career, prosperity, longevity, and energy.

China's Jade Culture

Visitors to China are invariably exposed to various gift items made from jade, and knowing something about the extraordinary role that jade has played in Chinese history is a big advantage. The Chinese have revered and treasured jade for more than five thousand years.

Confucius himself wrote about the eleven virtues of jade:

> The wise have likened jade to virtue. For them, its polish and brilliancy represent the whole of purity; its perfect compactness and extreme hardness represent the sureness of intelligence; its angles, which do not cut, although they seem sharp, represent justice; the pure and prolonged sound, which it gives forth when one strikes it, represents music. Its color represents loyalty; its interior flaws, always showing themselves through the transparency, call to mind sincerity; its iridescent brightness represents heaven; its admirable substance, born of mountain and of water, represents the earth. Used alone without ornamentation it represents chastity. The price that the entire world attaches to it represents the truth.

Because jade represents beauty, grace, and purity, it has been used in many Chinese idioms and expressions about beautiful things. *Yu*, the ideogram for jade, is often used in women's names. In addition, Taoism's supreme deity is called Yu Huang Dadi (the Jade Emperor).

Traditionally, jade has been made into tools, ornaments, utensils, and many other items. It was also popularly made into sacrificial vessels and was buried with the dead. The body of Liu Sheng, ruler of the Zhongshan State (d. 113 BC), was buried in a jade burial suit composed of 2,498 pieces of jade sewn together with gold thread.

Part III

Doing Business in China

Chapter 6

Foreigners and the Chinese Way of Doing Business

In the 1960s and 70s when foreign companies first began going into Japan their top executives generally chose to do so in the form of joint ventures, because they didn't know anything about how business was done there. Most of them lived to regret this because the goals and procedures of the two sides were so different that the relationships often turned sour within the first year. After three to five years, some of these companies gave up and left, some started over from scratch, and others bought their partners out. This pattern was to be repeated in China some 30 years later.

By 2005 it was becoming more and more obvious that foreign companies doing business in China would ultimately be better off if they did so on their own. A growing number of companies involved in joint ventures began taking steps to convert them to Wholly Owned Foreigner Enterprises (WOFE), and more and more newcomers began taking the WOFE route from the beginning.

It is obvious that knowledge about China's business etiquette and skill in using it is far more important for these WOFE than joint-venture operations—and that this importance is not going to diminish in the foreseeable future. In fact, some of the biggest problems facing foreign companies wanting a presence in China are their failure to study the country's culture and history and a general lack of advance preparation.

"Many seem to assume that doing business in China is basically no different than in their home country, and all they have to do is show up and start the process," said one veteran consultant on doing business in China.

In reality, preparations for a startup business in China should begin as many as two or three years before the proposed starting date.

This period can be dramatically shortened by retaining experienced consultants, but it is remarkable how often this simple step is ignored by foreign companies. And it seems that the larger the company, the more likely they are to assume that they don't need any outside help.

Wisely choosing the person who will head up proposed China operations is a vital part of doing it right. The individual should have experience in China or have strong background education in its culture and language. He or she should be old enough to interface with age-sensitive officials and managers. Also important is a well-balanced personality, extraordinary patience, and a knack for dealing with people in contentious situations.

Going into China cold is not a good idea. It pays to have one or more introductions. If you do not have any personal contacts in your own country or in mainland China there are obvious sources for professional help, including consultants, chambers of commerce, China's international trade offices, and so on. It is also an excellent idea to make a preliminary trip to Hong Kong or Shanghai to tap into the numerous resources that are available in those cities.

The obvious first step that foreign nationals who want to do business in China should take is to determine whether or not their country has a chamber of commerce in the People's Republic of China. The United States, for example, has chambers of commerce in Beijing, Shanghai, Guangdong, and Hong Kong, and a smaller branch chamber in Tianjin. These chambers provide a plethora of services to their members, including a regular China brief, regulatory alerts, China business insight, and government relations resources. They also provide local living guides, travel information, and lists of health-care services, international schools, community groups, alumni associations, and both domestic and foreign media. Other national chambers of commerce in China provide a similar list of services to their business communities.

The Changing Role of Foreigners in the Workplace

After the Communist take-over in 1949, comparatively few foreigners travelled to China for work, business, tourism, or study, and those that did came mostly from the Soviet Union or Soviet-block countries. This trickle came to a near standstill after China split from the Soviet

Union in 1960, and the country was all but closed to the outside world during the Cultural Revolution. The small group of foreigners who remained in China during that time were for the most part treated as spies, and some even spent time in prison.

After 1979, China opened up once again for tourism, for study, and for expatriates wanting to work or do business. However, there were great restrictions placed on their movements and activities. Typically, foreign workers and businessmen pretty much lived in special hotels or guest houses that had been set aside for them. And, only Chinese citizens were allowed to posses and use China's currency, the RMB (*renminbi*). Foreigners had to use Foreign Exchange Certificates (FEC notes), which could only be spent at a handful of expensive restaurants and hotels, and at Friendship Stores—small department stores which mostly sold luxury items and imported goods. Chinese nationals were not legally allowed to shop at the Friendship Stores, and foreigners were not legally allowed to shop anywhere else. Of course, a healthy black market involving FEC notes and the RMB soon emerged, so foreigners could shop at local markets and Chinese could shop at Friendship Stores. This black market became so large and uncontrollable that the Chinese government finally abolished FEC notes in 1994.

Foreign workers in those days were generally called foreign experts, and had Foreign Expert Certificates (actually, a small book with their name and photo in it), and by and large they worked either directly for the Chinese government, at an SOE, or at a government school or institution. While they were often treated with honor by their Chinese hosts, their movements and activities were usually tightly limited. Typically, these foreign experts would find themselves isolated from their Chinese counterparts, as they answered directly to the Foreign Expert's Bureau and were under a different management than the Chinese staff. Many were under covert (or in some cases, not so covert) police surveillance. And, though their income might be several times that of their Chinese counterparts, by any Western standard it was exceedingly low. Indeed, until mid-2000, the state-mandated pay for most foreign experts was no more than US $250 a month, though this was mitigated by the fact that their housing—and sometimes their food—was provided for, and the work was often light to almost non-existent, with some foreign expert teachers putting in as little as ten hours of work a week.

In the late 1990s and early 2000s, things began to loosen up considerably for foreign workers in China, as increasingly many were able to find jobs at private companies or private educational institutions. Working and living conditions and salaries varied greatly from foreigner to foreigner, even within the same city. Some foreign experts saw little or no changes in their work or salaries. However, working conditions for foreigners in private employment varied from the horrid to the sublime. Some foreigners worked as virtual slaves for employers who kept their passports and limited their movements, while others worked with little or no supervision as managers with salaries ten to twenty times higher than the typical educated Chinese.

Since the Chinese workforce by and large lacked technical or managerial skills and foreign language ability, some lucky foreigners were able to parley their education or background into high-powered positions in private companies and SOEs, and even new university graduates from the US and Canada were in some cases able to get high-level management or technical jobs, though they lacked work experience or Chinese ability. Others were able to get rich by starting their own companies, either as joint ventures or WOFEs, or in many cases without proper licensing at all. These new foreigners were not under the authority of the Foreign Experts Bureau. They could live wherever they wanted, and were not under any kind of obvious police surveillance unless they went out of their way to court trouble. Finally, they no longer found themselves isolated from their Chinese co-workers, though the Chinese reticence to invite foreigners to their homes or become more than work acquaintances was—and still is—often a factor in daily life.

The situation gradually matured as the first decade of the twenty-first century wore on. The companies which treated foreigners as slaves discovered that they could no longer sponsor employment visas, and that the government was not going to tolerate foreigners working illegally on tourist or business visas. It became increasingly difficult to find technical or managerial positions without extensive experience and some Chinese language ability. And, many foreigners who had started their own businesses found themselves squeezed out of the market by Chinese competitors, shut down by the government, or both.

Increasingly, it has become a trend to favor hiring overseas Chinese or Chinese returnees for jobs that had previously been held by non-ethnically Chinese Westerners, and in fact the Chinese government is encouraging this tendency. Overseas Chinese are ethnic Chinese from the vast Chinese diaspora, which stretches from Hong Kong to London. While such Chinese may sometimes find themselves discriminated against when it comes to getting jobs at some English schools, because for marketing purposes these schools want to have a white face for a teacher, when it comes to technical or management jobs they often have an edge over other candidates, assuming that they have the experience and education. Chinese returnees are mainland Chinese who immigrated or went to study overseas, but who have come back to China to live and work. Many companies which previously hired Westerners now focus on hiring Chinese returnees.

For cost reasons and to placate the Chinese authorities, many Western companies have committed themselves to localizing their workforce by hiring ethnic Chinese. At the same time, in its rush to modernize, China has emphasized getting a university degree as a path towards financial success. However, it now has many more university graduates than it has well-paying jobs requiring university degrees. When all these factors are combined with an economy which has slowed in recent years, the job picture for foreign workers is very different now than what it was a decade ago.

At present, it is generally not even possible to get a work visa unless you have a university degree and two years of work experience outside of China in the field you are applying for. And, apart from jobs in education, most jobs require some Chinese speaking ability, with many jobs requiring Chinese fluency in both speaking and writing. Finally, unless you have years of experience or are quite lucky, getting hiring directly for a management position is in most cases out of the question—those jobs generally go to people who are ethnically Chinese.

The non-education related jobs that are available for foreigners at the moment are generally the same as those available to the Chinese, and foreigners often find themselves in direct and keen competition with the Chinese for these jobs. In 2005, there were several online job banks full of positions available only for foreigners in China. Most of these sites no longer exist and the ones that still do exist post comparatively few jobs, so a foreigner looking for work in China may have to resort to Chinese job sites. Long-term foreigners who were hired many years ago and have kept working at the same company may have salaries several times higher than their Chinese co-workers. This is typically no longer the case for foreigners just entering the Chinese job market—their salaries, working conditions, and statuses will often be comparable to that of a Chinese employee. However, since many of the companies that are willing to hire foreigners face outwards towards overseas markets, there are still opportunities for talented foreigners to quickly enter mid-management, if they know how to work with Chinese people and have the necessary skills and drive. At the same time, many foreigners have discovered that a glass ceiling now exists preventing them from rising above mid-management and into an executive position. This is even more true of many Western companies than it is of some Chinese companies.

As foreigners now generally work for private companies, they face long hours on the job. Though these companies tend to be results-driven, if you do not put in the same time as everyone else, you will not be seen as a team player. Many foreigners have found jobs at tech or Internet companies, as this is one area where foreigners most often have better resumes than Chinese candidates. Just like tech and Internet start-ups in the West, however, these companies are looking for solutions. A foreigner who can provide them answers will quickly become a rising star, while a foreigner without the skills or initiative may soon find himself out of a job.

As most high-level managers at companies within China are now ethnically Chinese, when working within a company in China it is important to discern the company's actual management structure and philosophy, rather than the official structure and philosophy. Traditional Chinese management is almost feudal in nature, with unclear lines of authority and communications, hidden alliances based upon *guanxi* or favors, hidden agendas, and even pay-offs and corruption. When working at such a company, it is best not to take anything at face value, but to wait and watch so that you can see who has the real authority in the company, and what the real business priorities are, and then adjust one's behavior accordingly. This kind of Chinese management system even exists in some Western companies which are theoretically committed to modernized, Western management techniques. The Chinese management may pay lip service to the goals and priorities of the parent company, while at the same time running the local branch as a feudal fief. At the same time, there are both Western and Chinese companies which are run just like any company one might find in the West, and with exactly the same rules and expectations. Further, some companies have a mixture of the two management systems.

While foreigners working in China must have valid visas or resident permits that allow them to work, for the most part they no longer have a special legal status separate from the Chinese when it comes to the labor law. Like Chinese workers, they pay into the Chinese pension system and have Chinese health insurance, and in many cases they have substantial legal protection, preventing companies from firing them or laying them off without paying severance. Of course, while they now have greater protection under the law than ever before, for the most part gold-plated expatriate pay and benefits packages no longer exist for foreigners getting hired in-country.

Foreigners working in China are no longer privileged and are no longer treated as though they are in any way special—they typically find themselves in the mix with everyone else. As such, they tend to see Chinese people when they are most relaxed and not on their best behavior for visitors. Instead of polite hosts who are vague and indirect, their co-workers will most often be brutally frank, openly critical of each other and those in authority, and fully willing to make their own personal opinions clear. If a meeting involves Chinese staff members, there can at times be raised voices and the appearance of heated arguments. Yet, after the meeting is over, when you ask why there was such a violent disagreement, the participants will explain that they were just having a friendly discussion.

For good or for ill, this is the real China that foreign experts twenty years ago may never even have had a glimpse of. Yet, foreigners who can accustom themselves to working in this environment can still find success, though they will have to up their game considerably compared to the previous generation of expatriates. It is simply no longer possible for a foreigner to come to China with no experience and Chinese ability, and find a comfortable job working ten or fifteen hours a week while being treated like a king.

Dealing with 56 Chinas!

Chinese employed in business and government as well as foreigners who are familiar with China continuously point out that there is not just one China, and not just a single Chinese culture. While there are notable cultural similarities among the regions of China, as well as among its individual provinces, each area is different enough from the others that generalizations seldom fit. This means that business strategies must be devised for the different areas.

One veteran Chinese businessman has said that there are 56 different Chinas, in reference to the country's 56 officially recognized ethnic groups. In addition, there are 31 provinces in China, and much to the surprise of some foreign businesspeople going there for the first time, they often behave more like independent countries. The level of competition among these provinces ranges from strong to cutthroat. Some even have barriers against doing business with other provinces. Others charge excise taxes on raw materials "exported" to other provinces.

Large cities such as Shanghai also have their own ways of doing things, including both regulations and customs. This makes it imperative that companies planning to do business in these cities are acquainted with all of the local requirements.

One useful way of understanding the differences between Chinese and Western approaches to doing business is to think of the Western way as direct and the Chinese way indirect. Generally speaking, the Chinese way of doing business is inconvenient and inefficient—something the Chinese themselves recognize. In fact, the Chinese are slowly but surely adopting Western ways of doing business.

Nonetheless, foreigners doing business in China must know a lot about Chinese culture and become adept at working within or around it. They must accept the idea that in China all business is personal, and proceed from that assumption. It is a much greater stretch for Westerners to try to do business the Chinese way than it is for the Chinese to do business the Western way. Westerners should not try to do so beyond reasonable limits.

China's Government as Big Brother

China is credited with having invented bureaucracy, and it continues to flourish there today in all of its various forms, not the least of which are communist principles and practices that continue to survive despite the capitalistic glow that often suffuses foreigners' images of China.

There are two major facets to successfully doing business in China. One consists of understanding the traditional patterns of etiquette and behavior that literally go back to the days of Confucius. The other is learning to work with not only the central government of the People's Republic of China (PRC) in Beijing, but also with other city and regional governments throughout the country.

This creates a great sea of conflicting interests. Foreign companies are very much like ships on this sea, forced to sail with the prevailing current—sometimes coming from Beijing and other times from local power centers. All levels of Chinese government are first dedicated to advancing their own economic and political interests, which generally involves stretching or altogether ignoring any obligations they may have—or may be considered to have by others—to what is often described as "fair trade."

Foreign businesses must also deal with the Chinese government in other ways. At one time, Chinese government-owned companies controlled the distribution of nearly 80 percent of all the goods sold in the country. Now with the growth of the private sector, this share has dropped to about 25%. However, the 12 largest Chinese companies are state-owned, as are the vast majority of the Chinese companies on Fortune's Global 500 list. Furthermore, it is said by people in the know that the People's Liberation Army (PLA) is the largest commercial conglomerate in the country, as well as its largest manufacturer of industrial and consumer goods. This means that foreign companies often cannot avoid doing business with one or more PLA-owned firms. Establishing and keeping good relationships with military leaders is therefore often more important than those involving private enterprises.

Confucius's precept that the more laws a government passes, the more people will disobey the laws led China's emperors to rule by decree rather than law. Laws have to go through a vetting process, while on a national level decrees can be issued by virtually anyone in a ministry or department of a ministry. On a local level officials and party bosses can issue decrees to their own liking. And this has been going on for well over two thousand years.

In addition, officials on all levels can interpret both laws and decrees as they see fit and whenever they want to. In effect, this means that individual officials in city and provincial governments have an enormous amount of leeway in how they do things. They can add a new tax, require a new form, delay or destroy applications, and so on.

This ancient system personalizes business and makes it inevitable that various forms of corruption will occur. If an official doesn't like you or has something against your company, he or she can stifle your efforts. Not surprisingly, some officials are more interested in personal gain than in benefiting their city or region, and this can present an especially sensitive situation.

Foreign businesspeople must learn how to swim in this sea, and the farther they get from Beijing and other big cities the more currents they must contend with. The answer to most of the challenges that confront foreign businesspeople in China is the personal approach. They must meet, impress, and build good relations with officials in all the sections, departments, and ministries that have anything to do with their area of business. As consultants on doing business in China repeatedly point out, business there is a people-to-people thing.

Another bureaucratic factor that slows things down in China is the habit of deferring decision-making to individuals on higher levels. In the past—and even today—it could be dangerous for lower-level officials to take any kind of responsibility. During the chaos of the Cultural Revolution, for example, common people had virtually no right to make decisions. Those who did risked being eliminated.

This traditionally made individuals wary of taking responsibility for even minor things and resulted in workers showing little or no initiative on their own. Even today, bureaucrats at nearly every level of government take the attitude that the best decision is no decision. And indeed, it is nearly impossible to punish a bureaucrat for not making a decision, even if it is integral to his job description. Bureaucrats are regularly punished for making wrong decisions, however. This means most power is centered at the top in Chinese companies and government organizations. As a result of this deeply entrenched custom, high-ranking officials are generally inundated with things requiring their attention. This can cause delays that can go on for days, weeks, or longer.

It is obviously not all gloom and doom for foreign companies in China; many of them are successful. Not surprisingly, some of the most significant foreign successes in China have been joint ventures with government-owned enterprises because they are unrivaled when it comes to having leverage with bureaucrats.

Layers of bureaucracy in inland and northern areas continue to make doing business a serious challenge. The existing central and local laws that must be obeyed—or circumvented—in order to get anything done are only part of the problem. That having been said, a great many of the communist-inspired bureaucratic controls from both central and local governments have been eliminated or greatly reduced since the 1980s and 90s, particularly in the Special Economic Zones in the south and other areas that are allowed considerable leeway in how they operate.

In spite of some seemingly counterproductive traditions, the central government of the People's Republic of China is obviously determined to restore the country to its ancient position as the Middle Kingdom, and it is just as obviously well on its way to accomplishing that goal. Local governments have their own interests at heart, and while they typically ignore policies and laws adopted by the central government or change them to suit their purposes, they too are making extraordinary contributions to the growing economic power of China.

The Language Barrier

Language is one of the most fundamental difficulties faced by Western business in China. In the past the government deliberately used the Chinese language as a barrier to help keep foreigners at bay. There is still a significant level of paranoia about keeping foreigners at arm's length, but the language is no longer used as a deterrent.

But despite this, the language itself (or more correctly, the languages themselves, since ten languages are spoken in the country) continues to be a major obstacle for foreign businesspeople. Overcoming the language barrier—or at least diminishing it until it's surmountable—requires some foreknowledge and the use of common sense: Make sure you have your key presentation materials translated by a professional into Chinese in advance. Retain the best interpreter you can find and afford. Go over every detail holistically. Continuously question the other side to make sure they understand and accept every point in any negotiations or contracts. Never take anything for granted. Don't get impatient and make concessions for which you get nothing in return. And most important, always remember that successful business relationships in China are like marriages—they are very personal and require constant give-and-take by both parties.

The Culture Barrier

It goes without saying that dealing successfully with the Chinese in business, diplomatic, and political affairs requires an extraordinary level of knowledge about Chinese culture, ranging from people's day-to-day customs to their deepest beliefs and motivations.

This situation is further compounded by the fact that the Chinese are extraordinarily sensitive to body language, facial expressions, and casual remarks that Westerners toss off without thinking. Westerners should even be wary of simple smiles: The Chinese automatically distrust people who smile a lot in formal situations such as business meetings. They look on it as an indication that the person is insincere and not trustworthy. Contrast this with the Western interpretation of smiling as a sign of goodwill, respect, and that they are friendly and anxious to develop a good, mutually beneficial relationship. The problems that can and do arise in China from this seemingly innocuous cultural difference can be disastrous. In both business and personal situations in China, smiling is often a sign of embarrassment and care should be taken not to misinterpret it. Chinese people often smile when asked a question they can't or don't want to answer, or are put on the spot some other way.

The culture barrier in China is typically made more serious because Westerners, particularly Americans, want to do things quickly. They tend to work on precise timetables: five days in Beijing, three or four solid meetings, and bang, the deal is done.

The Chinese are not programmed to make decisions quickly, and attempts to force them to do so, wittingly or unwittingly, invariably backfire. Instead, they view things from all angles, over and over again, and while doing so make judgments about the sincerity and trustworthiness of the people they are dealing with. The more impatience Westerners demonstrate, the less trustworthy they are judged to be. At the same time, in many cases it would be wise for foreigners to view Chinese people who cater to that impatience—guaranteeing quick results or profit—with equal suspicion. Chinese businesspeople who are on the level tend only to engage in substantial or important transactions with people whom they have worked with over a long period of time on smaller deals, or in long series of small, confidence-building steps. As this is the way seasoned Chinese businesspeople behave with their own countrymen, why should Westerners behave any differently when in China?

Obviously there are, and should be, reasonable time constraints on business negotiations. The challenge is to discern what is reasonable from what is unreasonable. Some of the most conspicuous foreign successes in China have come about only because the companies involved took several years to maneuver themselves into the marketplace. By the same token, many of the most conspicuous failures were the result of going into the market too fast and doing it in the wrong way.

Part of the difference between Chinese and Western thought and behavior is expressed in the phrase *budan xin* (boo-dahn sheen), which means something like "sincerity plus understanding," although I believe it would be more accurate to reverse these two concepts, with understanding coming first.

In its Chinese context, this "understanding" refers to the foreigner understanding a situation from the Chinese perspective, to the depth and breadth that the Chinese do. "Sincerity" refers to the requirement that foreigners conform completely to the expectations and standards of the Chinese way, that is, of all the personal, social, and legal obligations that make up the foundation of Chinese behavior. To the Chinese, a sincere person is one who can be depended on to do what is right and expected from the Chinese viewpoint, regardless of the situation.

This combination of understanding and sincerity is the foundation of Chinese behavior, whether or not it makes sense to foreigners. And this is why the Chinese are continuously reminding foreigners that they must understand China in order to deal effectively with its people. It is also why the Chinese typically accuse foreigners of not understanding China when things go wrong. The Chinese believe that foreigners cannot be sincere in their relationships with Chinese if they do not understand China, since sincerity without understanding is impossible.

Like Americans, if I may make the comparison, the Chinese almost always automatically take the position that they are right and their way of doing things should prevail. It is therefore very important for foreigners dealing with China to be aware of the *budan xin* cultural factor and prepared to deal with it.

Understanding and dealing with commercial enterprises and government agencies in particular looks entirely different from the Chinese perspective. Almost nothing is thought of in the straightforward, expedient steps that logical and law-oriented Westerners expect.

I suggest that in the beginning of business or diplomatic relationships foreigners mention to their Chinese counterparts that they are familiar with the role of *budan xin* in Chinese culture because it is also an integral part of their own culture. At the same time they should note that there may be differences of opinion that will require both sides to compromise to achieve their goals. This will alert the Chinese that you know something about China, and provide you with a more solid footing for negotiating with them.

Professional Education & China's Political Culture

As emphasized by the many linguistic, cultural, and political differences between China and the West, it is important—and often absolutely necessary—for businesspeople to be fluent in both China's social and political culture.

This is unlikely to change in the near future. There is, in fact, some resistance and resentment in China to the common belief that the Western way of doing business is the best for China as well, and there are growing efforts to offer alternative methods of doing business.

Foreign educational institutions that offer special programs on doing business in China are growing in number, while universities and private organizations in China are increasingly offering degrees in international business. These latter institutions point out, and rightly so, that the business courses on China provided by foreign schools do not always address all of the key elements involved in doing business in China, or get right the ones they do. People who go through American MBA programs often have exceptional difficulty adjusting to the realities they discover in China.

There are predictions that Chinese schools offering MBA programs will close the gap between themselves and American schools as employers in China become more attuned to the local situation. Some international executive search firms in the United States have seen the writing on the wall and expanded their searches to Chinese schools. A number of American schools have opened branches in China.

At the same time, executives who are in the most demand are ones who have had both Chinese and foreign-style MBA training. It is also noted that even the most astute and successful Chinese entrepreneurs are limited when it comes to competing in the international business arena.

However, the number of young Chinese executives who opted to study abroad began dropping in direct proportion to the growth of the Chinese economy, as fears set in about losing their contacts and networks and not keeping up with their stay-at-home contemporaries.

Given the ongoing growth of its economy it is believed that China will need an additional five to six thousand new internationally trained executives every year for the foreseeable future. According to executive search firms in the United States and Europe, this will propel the growth of MBA programs in China and result in more foreign schools opening branches there.

The Dossier Factor in Chinese Life

Another practical aspect of hiring workers in China is the use of dossiers. Foreign companies operating in China may have to deal with an employment agency and the ancient Chinese practice of keeping detailed information about people. There is a *dang'an* (dahng-ahn), or personal dossier, on virtually every Chinese in the country. These are kept as the property of the schools they attend and the places where they work. Individuals have absolutely no rights to access the files that are kept on them.

When people want to change jobs their new employer requests a copy of their dossier from their old employer. If the old employer refuses for any reason to release the dossier the new company cannot legally hire the individual.

In Beijing alone there are five employment agencies whose primary function is to store the *dang'an* of the people on their rolls and contract them out to companies needing new employees. One of these five agencies is the Foreign Enterprise Service Corporation (FESCO), which specializes in providing employees for foreign companies. FESCO determines the official salary that foreign companies are required to pay the employees it places and takes part of this amount as its fee.

These agencies hold dossiers, which contain evaluation reports as well as other normally confidential information, over the heads of the workers on their rolls and often compel them to give up certain benefits they would ordinarily receive.

Women in the Business World

It is also worth noting that, thanks in large part to Mao Zedung, Chinese women have come a long way since the early days of the Communist regime. Mao was enlightened enough to understand that women are as important as men in society, and deserve the same economic, political, and social opportunities.

Women now play significant roles in virtually all areas of life in China, particularly in the economy, and there is little if any discrimination against foreign businesswomen. It is, in fact, common for Chinese businessmen to go beyond the norm in treating foreign businesswomen courteously and favorably.

The only rule is that women who behave in a professional manner will be regarded and treated as professionals.

Social Etiquette in Chinese Business

The term "etiquette" as it is known and used in the Western world is not deep or broad enough to encompass all of the cultural factors that pertain to the Chinese way of doing business. In China these factors go well beyond social conventions having to do with meeting, greeting, and interacting with people in routine situations such as dining together. They go down to the heart of all the cultural things that shape and define the Chinese character.

The Chinese are a proud people and because of the distinctive social and political systems under which they lived for millennia they are extraordinarily sensitive about their face—that is, their reputation, the way they perceive themselves and the way others perceive them—which has a direct influence on the way they do business.

As everyone knows, dramatic cultural changes have been underway in China since the last years of the 1970s. These changes have been and still are affecting people from every walk of life in China, particularly the millions who are now personally involved in international business and international affairs.

But despite these changes, including those that have westernized much of the country's facade, from its high-rise buildings to the way its people dress, the age-old culture of China is still powerful enough to control the thinking and behavior of most Chinese.

Social etiquette will only get you through the first two or three steps in initiating business dealings in China. Once you're past the front door and through the first few preliminary get-acquainted meetings deeper understanding is required. From that point on you need knowledge of the values and motivations of the Chinese individuals you are dealing with and the interests of the government, as well as considerable skill in getting your point across and even more skill in correctly interpreting Chinese behavior.

Virtually all of the many failures experienced by foreign companies attempting to do business in China were caused by problems understanding and dealing effectively with the intricacies of Chinese culture. For example, the American way of negotiating is almost completely the opposite of the Chinese way. Americans are individualistic, aggressive, and fact-and-truth oriented. The Chinese act as a communal team, their approach is to probe with indirect questions, and they exhibit more interest in how things are going to be done than in what is going to be done.

In the *Harvard Business Review on Doing Business in China* the team of John L. Graham and N. Mark Lam charted the cultural differences that separate Chinese and Americans (with Americans representing extreme Westerness). Their comparisons of basic cultural values and ways of thinking strips both sides of their surface facades: Americans are individualistic while the Chinese are collectivist. Americans are egalitarian while the Chinese are hierarchical; information oriented rather than relationship oriented; reductionist rather than holistic;

sequential rather than circular; and truth seekers rather than way seekers. The Americans take a debate approach to business, while the Chinese take a haggling approach.

Graham and Lam also detailed differences between the American and the Chinese way of negotiating: Americans prefer fast meetings and the Chinese prefer a long courting process. Americans like informal settings while the Chinese like formal settings. Americans use cold calls rather than the Chinese tradition of finding go-betweens.

In exchanging information Americans generally have full authority, while the Chinese have limited authority. Americans are direct; the Chinese are indirect. Americans invariably start out with proposals while the Chinese start out with explanations. Americans are aggressive; the Chinese are questioning. Americans are impatient; the Chinese are patient. American s strive for good deals; the Chinese strive for long-term relationships. Americans talk in straight lines; the Chinese talk in circles.

Regardless of how a foreign company enters China, there are still etiquette-based conventions that apply to doing business successfully—many of which are the same, or similar, to cultural do's and don'ts that apply in other countries.

To Succeed in Business You Must Have Face

China's unique history encouraged the importance of *mianzi*, or face, which is as vital for professional success as for personal. Businesspeople in China still have to develop and nurture extensive networks of personal connections with local and regional government officials and with suppliers to be successful. This need is one of the first things that foreigners wanting to succeed in China must understand.

Once they have established face and personal connections they must thereafter spend a substantial amount of time and money maintaining them. There are a variety of things involved in doing this, many of which are familiar to most people—eating and drinking together, giving gifts, doing favors, and so on. But these things must be done according to appropriate cultural protocol, or they may backfire.

It is also fairly common for Chinese to take personal advantage of those who need their friendship and cooperation, especially naive foreigners, and these situations may be hard for foreigners to recognize and avoid.

Throughout China's history—including the heyday of the Communist regime—many bureaucrats made a regular practice of using their power to get personal favors for themselves or members of their families from people who needed their services. A favorite goal was getting help to send their sons abroad for university-level education and post-graduate study.

The best recourse is to get insights and guidance from a trusted Chinese friend or a foreigner who has been in China for many years, is well-versed in the face and connections factors, and can guide you around the pitfalls and in gaining face for yourself and giving it to others.

The Role of *Guanxi*

Like all of Chinese society, China's business community does not rest wholly on a foundation of impartial laws and customs that applies to everyone. In business life as in personal life, this necessitates the use of *guanxi* (gwahn-she), or "connections." When the Chinese contemplate starting a business enterprise, need to get something done after they are in business, or must resolve some issue or problem, their first thought is to seek help from people with whom they have *guanxi* and who are in a position to bring their influence to bear in helpful ways.

Of course, the concept and practice of *guanxi* includes an equally strong sense of mutual reciprocity, known as *hui bao* (whee bah-oh), or "social reciprocity." Fulfilling the obligations of *hui bao* is one of the most important ways the Chinese develop, nurture, and sustain their face. Failure to properly discharge social debts is regarded as one of the most dishonorable things a Chinese can do. People who disregard *hui bao* are regarded as uncultured.

Foreign businesspeople are invariably compelled to develop and use the *guanxi* system in order to succeed in China, and it pays to begin developing the necessary personal connections well before arriving in the country.

Western businesspeople are familiar with the importance of connections and networking, but *guanxi* does not only involve connections in the business world. It refers first of all to personal connections—including family members, relatives, classmates, teachers, and friends—and business contacts for whom you have done favors. These helpful connections form three kinds of networks: family networks, government networks, and business networks. When operating on a larger scale, one has to deal with all three of them.

A key factor in the existence and use of any network in China is that it is dynamic. Because networks are personal they change as people change. Those that remain consistent over long periods of time involve senior men whose face and authority are unquestioned. They are the new mandarins of modern China.

While more and more Chinese in the international business arena are trying to break away from dependence on *guanxi* to accommodate new relationships with foreigners, they still almost always exert serious effort to quickly establish the kind of obligatory social debts they are accustomed to having in all their social and business dealings.

The vital role *guanxi* networks play in Chinese business notwithstanding, these networks do not provide all the help and answers one needs to succeed in China. They are vital, but they are only part of the equation.

The Value of Introductions

Westerners are, of course, familiar with the role of introductions in both social and business affairs—a role that is roughly analogous to the use of *guanxi* in China. And like Westerners, the Chinese are likely to respond positively to introductions from someone they know, an organization that is important to them, or a famous figure.

Presenting letters of introduction from well-known business leaders, overseas Chinese, or former government officials who have dealt with China is an excellent way of showing both that you are a person of high standing and that you mean business.

Introductions go a long way toward establishing the personal relationship that is essential for the Chinese in their business affairs.

The Information Black Hole

The overall Chinese market has been described as an information black hole because of a scarcity of reliable information, which is only exacerbated by the differences between China's 31 provinces and 56 ethnic groups.

On both national and provincial levels things that would be public knowledge in the West are deliberately kept secret by officials who treat it as insider information and make use of it to gain special advantages for their agencies and departments. This makes it necessary for Chinese as well as foreign companies to cooperate with these officials in order to attain access to and use this information—a situation that is likely to persist for the foreseeable future.

Using the Back Door in Business Relationships

There has always been a cultural disconnect between Chinese people and those who are not members of their inner circles. This especially includes employees of companies and government offices on all levels. In effect this means that clerks and officials in government offices—as well as employees of commercial companies and professional organizations—have traditionally never had any direct, specific obligation to serve the public. This is true even when that obligation would appear to be inherent in the purpose of their jobs.

This led a long time ago to the use of *hou men* (hoh-men), or "back doors," to get things done in China. As discussed in previous chapters, the first recourse of anyone who wants or needs something to be done in China is to search for a back door into the appropriate company or office—someone they themselves know or can contact through a family member or friend.

The practice of using *hou men* has been institutionalized in China for millennia, and continues to play an important role in virtually all areas of life in China, from getting a child into a certain school, finding a job, obtaining some kind of license or permission from a government office, getting out of trouble with the police, and so on.

Foreigners in China are often seriously handicapped until they have access to many back doors in their business areas.

Don't Rotate Managers

One of the worst things that Western firms in China do—particularly American ones—is rotating their foreign managers in China every three years or so. It takes from three to five years for the typical foreign manager to learn how to function effectively in China by developing a *guanxi* network, and so on. This rotation system, generally intended for the real or perceived benefit of the individuals involved, is a serious weakness in a firm's ability to succeed.

Instead, the best approach is to identify and train employees who are interested in making their careers in China. When they are ready to hang it up after twenty or thirty years, their replacements should already have been in place for at least three years, and preferably five.

Chapter 7

Cultural Influences Vital in Chinese Business

China's traditional business culture is rapidly becoming more practical, efficient, rational, and international. There is a danger in this, however, because the more capable the Chinese become in doing business the international way, the more competitive they will be. In general they are incredibly smart, hardworking, diligent, tenacious, and ambitious to a point that must be seen to be believed.

Foreign businesspeople who do not take this new future to heart and prepare themselves may end up working for the Chinese as junior partners.

The following cultural factors continue to influence professional behavior in China, and are invaluable for Western businesspeople to understand.

Business as Guerrilla Warfare

In the 1950s and 60s one of the bestselling books in Japan was *The Art of War*, a classic treatise written by the Chinese military strategist and tactician Sun Tzu in around 500 BC. Hundreds of thousands of Japanese businessmen bought and virtually memorized it not because they were bent on starting a new war, but because they were absolutely determined to succeed in business and instinctively related the conduct of business with that of war.

The extraordinary idea of using military stratagems and tactics taught by China's famed Sun Tzu to succeed in business obviously worked—in fact, the approach worked so well that in just 20 short years tiny, war-devastated Japan morphed into the world's second-largest economy.

Near the end of the 1970s when ordinary Chinese were allowed for the first time in their country's history to explore the dynamics of capitalism and the world marketplace, they used the principles and practices espoused in *The Art of War* in their approach to business even more naturally than the Japanese had. By 1980 the Chinese associated these stratagems of war with achieving success in business, particularly when they were dealing with foreign companies that could easily be viewed as the enemy.

Today virtually all Chinese businesspeople are skilled in the use of "war" strategies and tactics in their conduct of business because it is embedded in their culture to do so.

This pragmatic approach to business often provides the Chinese with advantages in their dealings with Americans and other foreigners whose concept of business is generally one-dimensional, and therefore limits what they do and how they do it. The emergence of China as an economic superpower in less than three decades validates equating war with both politics and business. This is a lesson especially appropriate for the United States, where the prevailing culture tends to view and treat war, politics, and business as separate entities.

I recommend that foreigners dealing with China—in business as well as in political affairs—be thoroughly versed in Sun Tzu's guidelines. Especially key among Sun Tzu's precepts is that the general must know everything there is to know about the enemy and be prepared to both anticipate and adapt to changing circumstances as they occur. This requires up-to-the-minute intelligence, knowledge of one's own strengths and weaknesses, and an understanding of when and how to take advantage of any given circumstances.

For Western businesspeople, this means knowing enough about the mindset and plans of their Chinese counterparts to anticipate their actions and have strategies and tactics ready to deal with them.

The Senior/Junior Factor

The hierarchy-based system espoused by Confucius is still very much the order of the day in China. People are categorized by their social class, gender, age, position, and seniority. Although the Cultural Revolution temporarily turned this upside down, with youths of high school or university age functioning as militias charged with the responsibility of eliminating the Confucian ethic, hierarchy returned to the fore as soon as the revolution ended.

Broadly speaking, the hierarchical structure of China begins with sex and age: Men automatically outrank women. The firstborn outranks other siblings. In schools sophomores outrank freshmen in all respects, and so on up the educational ladder.

A person who becomes a teacher or an employee of any kind this year is senior to one who achieves this position the following year.

Employees of companies and government organizations are generally hired for specific work on the basis of their educational level, paid on the kind or class of their employment, and promoted on the basis of seniority. It is still rare for this hierarchical ranking to be ignored. A professor who outranks another professor by one year will almost always be the senior of the two. Likewise, government officials follow one another up the promotion ladder in a lockstep based on their seniority.

This system has long been the defining characteristic of Chinese society and continues today to impact virtually every aspect of Chinese life. Given its two-thousand-year history it is not apt to give way to the merit system anytime soon, despite the fact that some international companies in China do hire and promote on the basis of merit.

Regardless of whether a foreign company in China utilizes the merit system, considerable attention must be paid to the deeply ingrained hierarchy-based beliefs and feelings of Chinese employees.

Chinese Business: The New Generation

There is a large generational difference between older and younger Chinese businesspeople. Older Chinese businesspeople often have a zero-sum outlook on life. They assume that there is only a finite amount of resources, and they take a win-lose attitude towards business negotiations. When one considers that until 1912, China was very much a feudal society, it is natural that this would be a traditional viewpoint within the country. However, socialist rhetoric also ties in with this worldview, and until very recently nearly all government policy was predicated on zero-sum considerations.

Further, older Chinese grew up in circumstances of great lack. When combined with their zero-sum view of the world, their experience of privation tends to make them quite cautious with the resources they have, and to focus on the actual rather than the potential.

In many cases, their experience with the world outside of China may be slim to non-existent, and so they prefer to stick with traditional ways of doing business, in large part because this is what they know and trust. They also prefer to stay with what they think is the tried and true. Very often, this means following the pack and only investing in the same thing everyone else is investing in, or listening to the advice of highly respected businesspeople when making decisions. Sadly, this is not always a good business strategy.

All these factors can make older businesspeople quite hesitant to enter into new business deals, especially with a foreigner. And, when they do enter into a deal, the main draw for them is often the money they will receive when the deal is closed, and not any potential future profit from the investment. Indeed, some older businesspeople are so pessimistic that they may not care much at all about the project after the agreement is made—so long as they have made their initial profit they will be happy. Alternately, they may be happier to serve as a middleman for a deal rather than a principal, as this way they can make money coming and going, without exposing themselves to any risk. Many times too, older businesspeople will tend to get involved in business deals not because they expect to receive financial gain, but because they feel obligated out of *guanxi*, or because it will allow them to gain face.

Such traditional attitudes are still quite strong within China, even among young people. However, there is also a new breed of Chinese businesspeople who do not follow by the old rules and do not share the old expectations. This new breed came of age when the Chinese economy was growing by leaps and bounds, and may have never experienced poverty. Many in this group have been educated overseas or in private Western-style schools within China, and so they have a ready familiarity with the Western culture and way of doing business. In their lifetime, China has seen constant improvement, and many Chinese have become rich. Consequently, this new breed does not have a zero-sum view of the world, and is generally optimistic about change and the future. Instead of thinking win-lose, they tend to think in terms of win-win, and are more willing to take risks on deals where there may be low initial returns but great long-term rewards. They are also more willing to buck perceived wisdom and invest their time and energy in cutting-edge businesses, rather than merely following the pack.

Many prefer to deal directly, one-on-one, and eschew middlemen. Further, they are often more interested in measurable rewards than they are in intangibles such as prestige or face. At the same time, they feel a very strong obligation to their extended family, and at times may feel forced to agree to business deals which in the end may be detrimental to themselves, because it will help out a relative. In many senses then, they have a more Western outlook on business and life, while being fairly in tune with the realities of the Chinese culture and traditions.

Some of this new breed have become successful and even world-famous entrepreneurs. Perhaps the sterling example would be Jack Ma, the founder of the e-company Alibaba, and China's richest man. Ma started out as an English teacher, and only first went online when he was in his mid-thirties. He strongly believes in trying new things and taking risks to build one's personal dream, while keeping long-term goals at the forefront. As he said in 2009,

> As business leaders and entrepreneurs, we always have to ask ourselves: Why did we build this business? As companies grow and become public, most start to forget about their initial dreams, about why they built the company in the first place, which was to contribute to society and to help customers. Those are their real dreams, and not to produce good quarterly results. Good quarterly results are good, of course, but that's not the purpose of business. That is the by-product and result.

This is the kind of statement any number of Western entrepreneurs might have made.

Many of this new breed are managers in companies, and the fastest growing private companies typically have a member of this new breed as a CEO. Such CEOs may at times be even more ambitious and aggressive in seizing new opportunities and markets than their Western counterparts.

Yet, many others are mid-managers at private companies or SOEs. Since they have a strong interest in the West and in helping their country modernize and change, they often serve as liaisons with foreign visitors. This can cause problems, however, as in many cases they may be working for more traditionally minded supervisors. While they may be highly enthusiastic about a new idea or project, the project may meet stern resistance from their boss. So, the foreign businessman might think that everything is going ahead full steam, only to discover suddenly that there are unforeseen roadblocks, and his liaison may be unwilling or unable to tell him why these road-blocks exists.

Sooner or later, members of this new breed will be able to affect dramatic change within China. However, for the moment the tradi-tionalists still have quite a bit of power.

The Secrecy Syndrome

According to Confucius's teachings, it is easier to keep peace and harmony if laws are kept secret and standards of behavior are instead upheld though ritualized etiquette. This may have planted in Chinese culture the secrecy seed that was to grow into a national syndrome, not only throughout the government but also among the population as a whole.

Without a legal framework designed to prevent government excesses and guarantee human rights, the obligation for security and peace fell to clans, communities, and finally individual families. This environment turned keeping quiet and keeping things secret a national characteristic.

This heritage of secrecy is still very much alive in China on a governmental level, in private industry, and in families. In the latter case this generally involves things having to do with the authorities, and is particularly common in rural areas and among the smaller ethnic groups.

In addition, the hierarchical social system's etiquette impeded the sharing of information. It was taboo for a junior to question a senior about anything for any reason. And asking questions of juniors and one's peers could cause one to lose face, so was generally avoided. Further, asking questions of officials could literally endanger your livelihood, if not your life, as well as those of your family.

Even today employees will typically not ask questions or bring up subjects they believe might upset their superiors, and will keep quiet about things that should be questioned. This includes not asking questions about things they don't know how to do. The custom was, and still is to a considerable degree, to wait for superiors to give complete instructions.

This cultural heritage can pop up in unexpected places and at unexpected times, such as when visitors who don't know any better ask questions about things that would be routine in other countries. Where business questions are concerned, the only recourse is to diplomatically seek their answers in roundabout, informal ways.

Two-Dimensional Thinking vs. Three-Dimensional Thinking

Veteran China consultant Charles Lee has described the difference between Chinese and Western thinking by saying that the Chinese think in three dimensions while Westerners think in two. Westerners see things as they appear in "flat" movies, while the Chinese see things in the round, as if they are wearing 3-D glasses. The challenge is for the two sides to develop "cultural glasses" that allow them to see into their respective dimensions and come to an equitable compromise.

In the West, people are programmed to think in straight lines, proceeding from specific facts and logical suppositions that lead to precise, predictable conclusions. The Chinese have known for ages that things don't always work that way. They learned long ago that things occur in cycles that are more or less like circles, and that if you do not take into account all of the varied, often unpredictable, possibilities problems are likely to arise.

The ability to extrapolate how this influences the thinking and behavior of both parties is, of course, a reflection of the understanding of the two cultures.

Production vs. Consumption

It used to be said that the Chinese tended to emphasize production while Westerners emphasized marketing and consumption patterns. This was certainly true before the policy of reform and opening up was instituted in the late 1970s, when all industry was subjected to state planning and had to fulfill government production quotas. And, this is still true even today with many government institutions and SOEs, which are often focused on make-work projects in order to justify their payroll, without regard to quality or market demands.

Some of this attitude still lingers in China even in private enterprise, especially among less educated, lower-level workers. Indeed, quality control is perhaps the biggest issue facing anyone wanting to set up a factory in China, as the kinds of workers factories can normally afford to hire are likely to place a low priority on making products anyone anywhere would ever want to buy or use.

At the same time, since 2000, China has been rapidly transforming into a consumer-driven society, especially when it comes to manufactured goods. Now, the Chinese government has made it a national priority to boost consumption in the tourism and services sectors as well. The government hopes that this emphasis on consumer spending will keep the engine of economic growth going even as exports fade.

What this means in practice is that the workforce in many cases needs to be retrained and come to grips with the new economic realities facing China. However, when it comes to private companies, marketing and sales are as cutthroat and competitive as ever. Further, Chinese consumers are becoming increasingly picky and harder to please. This emphasis on consumption has also driven increased wages and increased expectations for most Chinese people.

Foreign firms wanting to do business within this new environment will need to have their fingers hard on the pulse of China's ever-changing consumption trends and marketing demands.

Collective Well-being

Foreigners doing business with the Chinese should keep in mind that the concept of collective well-being is uppermost in their minds, and that this will have a profound influence on their behavior.

Business relationships the Chinese will accept must contribute to their collective well-being, and the benefits of these relationships must be obvious. Furthermore, the relationship must benefit not only the commercial goals of the Chinese company, but also related government ministries and China itself.

The imperatives of contributing to collective well-being are among the most important reasons why the Chinese are so committed to long-term survival and viability. Their concern is generally that they survive whether or not a foreign partner does.

Foreigners are well-advised to keep this point in mind and to emphasize the long-term prospects of the relationship they are proposing.

Group Orientation vs. Individualism

The group orientation of the Chinese has lasted for millennia and continues to be a major factor in all aspects of life in China—from family relationships to approaches to projects and work in general. This has both a positive and a negative impact on most areas of Chinese life.

On the positive side, the Chinese are emotionally, intellectually, and spiritually programmed to work in cohesive groups that are generally not slowed down or otherwise affected by disagreements and lack of cooperation. Obviously, many endeavors lend themselves to a closely knit team effort, and in that respect the traditional group orientation of the Chinese has been a major advantage.

But this advantage has lost a great deal of its power in the new, competitive, market-based, capitalistic economy because it works well only when people are empowered to act individually.

In fact, one of the biggest problems China faces today is finding ways to dramatically reduce the hold group orientation has on its people and to reeducate them to think and behave individually. Doing this is not as easy as it may sound to Western ears.

A major obstacle in this process is China's educational system. The educational system of China has been heavily influenced by Confucian ideas, which emphasized the rote memorization of classical texts without regard to application or meaning. After 1949, the Chinese government employed the Soviet model, wherein all education was centrally directed from Beijing, with the emphasis on literacy, practical sciences, vocational skills, and socialist rhetoric. In this, the goals of the government were not to produce critical thinking or creativity among the people, but to produce good communist workers and citizens. This means conformity, and not individuality.

Public education came to a complete standstill during the Cultural Revolution. However, when it was revived once again in the late 1970s, the government set a goal to have a fully literate society. As most people did not have access to even primary education before the Cultural Revolution, to fulfill this new goal the government had to open thousands of new schools and employ untold thousands of new teachers.

Even today, there is a dire shortage of well-trained teachers, materials and facilities, especially in rural or poorer areas. Given that there are typically more than 60 students per class in Chinese primary and secondary schools, rote learning is the norm, as there are simply not enough resources for much else. Indeed, the main focus is on literacy, and it is questionable whether it is even possible to become fully literate in Chinese without rote memorizing several thousand Chinese characters.

Added to this is the pressure of the dreaded *gaokao* exam. The *gaokao* (gah-oh-kah-oh) is the exam Chinese high school students must take and pass if they hope to go to a university. A university education is seen by most people in China as the key to wealth and prosperity, not just for the person taking the exam, but for the entire family, so a lot rides on this test. Yet, because the test was instituted in the late 1970s, when very few people in China saw education as anything but rote memorization, the *gaokao* requires little or no critical thinking skills or creativity to pass. It is primarily a test of rote-memorization skills.

While there is great pressure within China to change the education system so that it focuses on critical thinking, individuality, and creativity, and de-emphasizes rote memorization and conformity, this change cannot occur without a change in the *gaokao*. However, students in rural and poorer schools would be hurt by such a change, as they do not have access to the necessary trained teachers and resources. Further, the Chinese government still sees the primary purpose of education as producing good communists workers and citizens, and this conflicts with the goals of education reform. For these reasons, it is unlikely that there will be any wholesale changes in the Chinese education system soon.

This lingering group orientation of the Chinese naturally has an impact on foreign companies operating in China. Many companies, particularly those involved in marketing and selling locally, are at a serious disadvantage when they cannot find people who think and behave as individuals. Some of them now run their own schools to teach their employees to think independently and self-motivate.

The new focus of China's most progressive high schools and colleges is the need for students to break away from the traditional system of rote learning and learn how to think and act as individuals. With every step toward this goal, across-the-board changes in China will be even more dramatic than what has occurred in the recent past. I would expect a tipping point to be reached well before the middle of this century.

China's Emphasis on Self-sufficiency

The Chinese have traditionally been under enormous pressure to be totally self-sufficient; they could not depend on any government entity or people other than family and close relatives to help them, to take care of them in good times or bad.

This is what drives present-day Chinese companies (and ministries, and the Chinese military) to be as self-sufficient as possible. Unless foreigners are aware of this imperative they cannot fully understand the mentality and behavior of their Chinese counterparts, and cannot deal with them with maximum effectiveness.

This vital difference between Chinese and foreign companies—as well as China's government and foreign ones—must be taken into account if the built-in friction between the ways of the Chinese and the ways of foreigners are to be kept under control.

Personal vs. Group Accountability

When trying to understand the differences in mindset between Chinese business managers and government officials and Westerners, one should keep in mind that Westerners typically feel empowered to make decisions and to force change on their own initiative, while Chinese people typically do not.

From a historical perspective, this is completely understandable. In the Western world, individual actions have historically entailed risks, but also rewards. And, while the rewards may be great, the main risk is failure. After you fail, you can always dust yourself off and try again.

This has never really been true in China. Historically in China, the personal rewards for individual initiative have nearly always been small to non-existent, while the penalties for failure were often draconian and harsh, and could be imposed upon not just the individual, but on everyone related to him. For this reason, many Chinese try to avoid being personally accountable, and seek to take refuge in the safety of group accountability, because if everyone is guilty it will be impossible to single out one individual for blame and punishment.

Except in rare and relatively recent cases Chinese businesspeople do not have individual responsibility for their actions, and they will not try to take it. Theirs is a world of mutual responsibility, and one that works primarily on a consensus basis. Westerners, on the other hand, tend to be individualistic to the extreme, and many are simply incapable of working as total team members.

Even those fabled Chinese tycoons who built and ran great conglomerates did not do it on their own. Today, they are surrounded by family members who devote their lives to supporting their enterprises. And unlike Western tycoons these fantastically successful businessmen generally keep a low profile and are often unknown to the public.

The difference between the mutual responsibility of the Chinese and the individual responsibility of Westerners has profound implications when it comes to negotiating and doing business together. Many of the points of friction that arise are so subtle that neither side focuses on them, sometimes allowing them to fester into serious problems. Other points of friction are so conspicuous the proceedings come to a loud, screeching stop.

There is no simple solution to these cultural differences. The Chinese cannot easily change their attitudes and behavior because they are deeply integrated into their whole cultural mindset and the structure of their organizations. They must act as a team or the whole structure falls apart.

Individualistic Westerners, on the other hand, can decide without causing disruption on any level that they are going to work as a team, not only among themselves but while interfacing with their Chinese counterparts. And this is the approach they generally must take to succeed in China.

Open-ended vs. Closed

While Chines people do indeed know and use the concept of "yes" and "no", they generally prefer to keep things open-ended and under negotiation, rather than to have matters settled and closed as would most Western businesspeople. For this reason, when it comes to negotiations many Chinese businesspeople would prefer not to give a quick "yes" or "no" answer. Instead, they often wish to take their time, look at things from every angle, clear up every and all possible ambiguities in the contract, and get the best possible deal for themselves.

At the same time, once a contract is settled, negotiations are truly over as far as most honest businesspeople are concerned, and one can expect little or no flexibility regarding contract terms. One will often get whatever was literally promised in writing in the contract, and nothing more. Many Chinese people can be exceedingly legalistic and even pedantic in this sense.

There are two huge caveats to this observation. First, since the Chinese are not stupid, if a businessman can get you to offer more than the contract states, or if he can get you to change the way contract terms are interpreted to be more favorable to himself, he might do so. However, it is highly unlikely that you can get the same concessions from him.

Second, while Chinese people traditionally see their word as their bond and take contracts quite seriously, until recently in modern China there has been little in the way of a legal framework for enforcing contracts, and the legal system is often (but not always) heavily tilted against foreign firms. This gives plenty of room for unscrupulous operators to abuse or even ignore contracts after they have been signed.

Having said all this, if you are doing business in China, you should know your Chinese counterpart well enough to be able to assume that he is operating in good faith. And, like him, you should not be so quick to offer up a "yes" or "no"—you should take your time when negotiating the contract. Also, keep in mind that there are legal remedies within China for enforcing a contract, and a Western company should not hesitate to pursue those remedies if it thinks it is being taken advantage of. While it is true that it might not get a fair shake in court, in many cases legal or administrative measures can nevertheless be applied and a satisfactory solution can be found.

Intellectual Piracy in China

The Chinese have no history of intellectual property rights. Both knowledge and technology have traditionally been considered public, not private. This attitude continues to persist, and is one of the primary reasons why counterfeiting has remained common and why many foreign companies have suffered serious losses.

This factor has played a significant role in China's rapid rise as an economic power. The government is acutely aware of these violations of intellectual property rights and has done little or nothing to stop them, which is one reason why they have continued to persist. Growth obviously comes before any serious attempt to change the culture.

When Deng Xiaoping started China on the road to a market economy in 1978, there was no legal system for settling business disputes. Even though the legal system has been greatly strengthened, in China, a local company may deliberately pirate some foreign product or technology, presuming that if they are caught the foreign company will have little or no legal recourse. The local company will then typically set up its own factory and become a competitor to the foreign firm. As the local firm may have marketing resources and government officials on its side, it can in many cases squeeze the foreign firm out of the market, using the foreign firm's own IP against it.

In most cases, the main culprit is actually the foreign firm's joint venture partner. Indeed, the typical pattern is for a Chinese firm to joint partner with a foreign firm for no other reason then to gain access to the foreign firm's financial resources and IP. Once the Chinese firm receives the contracted payments and gains access to the IP, it will void the contract or, failing that, declare bankruptcy or even disappear. Even some Fortune 500 companies have been victimized by this, losing millions of dollars in the process.

This trend has become so rampant that most experts now advise foreign companies to go the WOFE route in China. Doing so allows them to limit access to their technology and marketing strategies.

Part IV

Negotiating in China

Chapter 8

The Chinese Way of Negotiating

The government regulations and requirements—both official and unofficial—that have traditionally made doing business in China toilsome and frustrating have, in fact, been significantly reduced since the 1990s and these barriers are continuing to come down.

In spite of this more hospitable business environment, there are still many stumbling blocks. Most foreign companies already doing business in China find their biggest ongoing challenges to be understanding and dealing effectively with the distinctive way Chinese businesspeople and government officials negotiate. This is also especially true of companies proposing to do business there. Hyperbolically speaking, the Chinese approach to negotiation is as different from the Western one as day is from night.

The overall process of Chinese-style negotiation is based on a precise number of cultural principles or themes that are characteristic of Chinese thought and behavior. Some of the most important of these themes are discussed in a number of key words already mentioned in this book, terms that I refer to as cultural code words, meaning they are impregnated with cultural meanings and uses that define the mindset of the Chinese.

In many ways, the most important of these key words refers to the self-image of the Chinese, often referred to as their "face."

The Power of Face

As mentioned in previous chapters, *mianzi* is generally translated as "face." This concept is well known in the West, but has far deeper and broader implications in China than in the Western world. One of the secrets to succeeding in business in China is to have a lot of face and avoid causing anyone else to lose theirs. In a negotiating session, for example, causing someone to lose face—especially one of the higher ups—can bring the whole thing crashing down. By the same token, giving face to the team or its important individual members can be a major asset.

It is important for Western businesspeople negotiating in China to understand that their face is a changeable thing subject to negative and positive fluctuation. Your face is subject to being increased or decreased by everyday events that would be ignored elsewhere. You can lose face if you don't succeed in a bargaining situation. You can lose face if a bank refuses you credit. You can lose face if someone below your status expects you to deal with him or her. You lose face if someone criticizes you. You lose face if someone insults you. You lose face if someone has damaged your face and you don't get revenge. These are things that people can do to you, deliberately or inadvertently, to make you lose face.

You gain face by making wise decisions. You gain face by succeeding at whatever you are trying to do. You gain face when someone publicly compliments or praises you. You gain face by making new, powerful friends, and so on. People also gain face by wearing designer clothes and eating in expensive restaurants—even when these indulgences strain their budgets.

To the Chinese, organizations and companies also have face. It is important to keep this in mind and be wary of doing anything that might cause them to lose face in the eyes of their people. You should also give them face when the opportunity arises. Criticizing a company or organization that you want—or need—to do business with can come back to haunt you.

Foreign negotiators often cause themselves and their Chinese counterparts to lose face by getting angry, sounding off loudly, or breaking a promise.

The Friendship Factor

In addition to other cultural factors that influence Chinese behavior, personal friendships that are warm and trusting are essential for success in business and are a factor in the Chinese way of negotiating.

Generally, the Chinese will not do business with people they don't know well because they understand that what will bind the two sides together is trust, not a contract. They therefore spend a significant amount of time trying to learn as much as possible about potential business partners before negotiating an agreement, and tend to grow relationships through small, confidence-building steps.

Foreign businesspeople should make this process as fast and as easy as possible by providing the Chinese side with extensive dossiers on their educational and professional background. These dossiers should include any previous experience they have had in China, and any notable Chinese contacts they may have.

From the moment the Chinese meet new people, particularly foreigners, they begin to measure their characters and personalities and the warmth and friendliness of their attitude toward them. This includes taking stock of their attitude toward China, and is therefore not something that can be done in a matter of minutes, hours, or even days. It can go on for weeks and is one of the reasons it takes a considerable length of time to negotiate business relationships in China.

Thinking Holistically

Instead of discussing projects and relationships in a straight line starting with A and ending with Z, the Chinese start anywhere between the two points, ignoring the linear progression that Westerners are conditioned to follow. This nonlinear approach resulted in the Chinese emphasis on what is now called holistic thinking.

During negotiations, this upsets the foreigners and leaves them in the dark about whether the talks are making progress. The only recourses they have for gauging their progress are after-hours meetings where they will have opportunities to ask one of the Chinese participants. Such off-the-record conversations can often be quite enlightening.

Facts & Truth vs. How Things Are Done

Western business is based on facts and truth; Chinese business is based on how things are done. This cultural difference can be a barrier during negotiations and while conducting business, but there is no fast, direct way around it. Getting past it is a matter of ongoing negotiation and finding solutions that both sides can accept.

Patience Is The Key

Many older Chinese businesspeople may much be less interested in finalizing a deal than their foreign counterparts. In some cases, the very fact that they are negotiating with a foreigner will help them build face, or help them make side deals with other Chinese people who unrelated to the negotiations. The negotiations themselves in some cases may be more valuable to them than the end results.

This is one reason why some Chinese do not feel any great sense of urgency to complete negotiations quickly, and instead sometimes continue with them for months or years. They have also learned from experience that lengthy negotiations result in foreigners giving away more and more in an effort to make a deal before they have to leave. A contract that proves them to be shrewd negotiators when it comes to foreigners can bestow upon them great face after the foreigner delegation leaves, so it is to their advantage to hold out for the best deal possible, no matter how long it takes.

Another factor that must be taken into account is that some Chinese pride themselves in stubbornly standing by their decisions, once those decisions are made. They might set certain goals before they enter into negotiations with a foreign firm, and will not conclude negotiations until these goals are met. If it looks like these goals will never be met, then it is to their advantage to continue negotiations indefinitely, as this will keep them from admitting defeat and losing face.

All of this is much less true of China's younger generation. Many have been Western educated or heavily influenced by the Western culture. Like their Western counterparts, they have bought wholeheartedly into the concept of time being money, and now suffer the same stress-related symptoms that are common in the United States and other countries. And, like their Western counterparts, they are often much more interested in concrete rewards than in intangible benefits such as prestige or face.

Never Forget; Never Forgive

The Chinese have been compared to elephants when it comes to remembering things; it has been said that they never forget and never forgive. The positive side to this is that favors done for an individual, family, or company are commonly remembered beyond the present generation and repaid when occasion arises. On the negative side, there is a growing tendency among younger Chinese to hold grievances against Britons, Americans, Japanese, and others for historical offenses against China. In truth, the Chinese government itself has been largely responsible for this trend, as since 1989 it has sought to foster an anger for foreign grievances in order to divert attention from its own shortcomings. This is one reason why foreign firms get short shrift in Chinese courts. It is very much an unwritten national policy to get foreign firms to pay for China's development as a recompense for past sins, real or imagined. And, if this means that sometimes foreign firms become victims of legal larceny, most Chinese would say this is justified.

The painful lessons of China's early exploitation by foreigners are still remembered today, and the Chinese often make use of them, subtly and otherwise, in the process of negotiations. The English may be reminded of the abuses their nation committed during the Opium Wars. Americans may be reminded that their nation's military forces invaded China in the late 1800s. The Japanese are reminded of the atrocities committed against the Chinese during the 1930s and World War II.

The British and Americans generally are not swayed by this attempt to shame them into being less demanding. The guilt-ridden Japanese, however, have been very susceptible and have accepted extraordinarily disadvantageous conditions in order to do business in China. By 2005 the growing importance of Japan as a source of investment and a market for Chinese-made goods had begun to mitigate the influence of this "victim card," at least on the governmental level. On visits to Japan, one Chinese leader after another made a point of announcing it was time to put the dark side of their shared history behind them. But that is not the end of the story.

The best response to comments about historical wrongs is to use diplomatic tactics to blunt or bypass the issue by pointing out the benefits that will accrue to China as a result of the relationship you propose.

Ultimatums Are Taboo

The Chinese do not react positively to ultimatums. They are, in fact, seen as challenges that may call for countermeasures. As such, it is best not to use them. It is nonetheless important to set negotiation deadlines of reasonable lengths—and to be willing to walk away if they are not met.

Keep in mind that if you do walk away they will lose face, so the threat of walking away can sometimes close the deal. However, this threat should only be used as a last resort, and you should realize that if you really do pull the plug on negotiations, you may have made yourself a sworn enemy, and may have ruined your own reputation in China. If you really want to walk away, but are afraid of the risks, a better tactic might be to simply let negotiations gradually peter out without having formally closed them.

Technology High on the List

Obtaining new foreign technology is high on the to-do lists of private and government-owned companies and government ministries in China. Just as the Japanese did in the 1950s and 60s, they regularly go into relationships with foreign companies primarily to obtain technology.

Foreign companies should weigh the gain versus the potential future loss before agreeing to such relationships. It often turns out that any gain is short-lived and any loss is dramatic.

Chinese negotiators commonly ask their foreign counterparts to toss some technology into the pot up front as a freebie. It is important to get something in return when agreeing to do this.

Chapter 9

Preparing to Negotiate in China

Over the ages, China's political, social, and economic environments have inured the Chinese to endure serious disadvantages and hardships, to work hard, and to persist in the face of great odds. In China this is referred to as *chiku nilao*, or "eating bitterness." It has resulted in the average Chinese person being extraordinarily diligent in their work and any other efforts they make.

Where negotiations are concerned, it is almost always the case that the Chinese side has worked harder and longer in preparation than the Western one has. The Chinese will also endure longer meeting sessions, ask more questions in more different ways, and demonstrate amazing patience with the pace of progress.

This makes preparation an invaluable tool for the foreigner negotiating in China. In particular, it pays to delve as deeply as possible—with great diplomacy—into any government regulations that might impact your goals and intentions. This must be done delicately, because if it becomes known that you are making such inquiries the ministry or agency concerned may order negotiations with you stopped.

Social Status Counts

The Chinese are extraordinarily sensitive to the social statuses of the people they deal with. Their status can be based on what regions of the country people come from, who their families are, where they went to school, their ages, their professional ranks, and so on. Chinese people are always conscious of this social status, and interact with others accordingly.

The value of status is so fundamental to Chinese society that individual Chinese companies and China's government take social status into account when hiring new employees or giving promotions.

Foreign businesspeople in China who are not aware of—or ignore—the status of their employees or who don't take status into account when dealing with business and government officials invariably cause friction that can be serious enough to damage or destroy a project.

One of the most common mistakes that foreigners make in their approach to business in China is sending someone there to represent them who is not old enough and does not have enough other qualifications to meet the standards of the Chinese. For example, a 50-year-old company executive or government official might consider it an insult if he or she is expected to deal with a 30-year-old. The Chinese would see such treatment as disregard for their status, as well as cultural ignorance and a blatant example of insincerity.

This makes it very important for foreign companies to put forth an effort to match the social statuses of negotiating teams they meet with and company executives with which they must interface.

Senior People & Negotiating

Senior staff in Chinese companies and government agencies typically do not take part in the negotiation process. They leave that to their staffs. If and when a senior person does show up it is usually an indication that the Chinese side has reached a consensus to formalize the relationship with a contract.

Senior people in foreign companies should not go to China to take part in negotiations from the beginning unless their companies are small and they have no one else who can adequately represent them. It is a hard and usually fast rule in China to match the rank and importance of people on foreign negotiating teams. This leaves them in a quandary when the president of a foreign company who is far below the rank of their own president shows up.

This problem can be avoided by providing the Chinese company with complete details about your company—its size, sales, and so on—and the members of your negotiating team. As mentioned before, the Chinese team will always expect to receive this kind of dossier.

Field the First Team

Chinese companies and governmental agencies prepare well in advance for negotiations, putting together teams of experts representing all areas of their organizations that are concerned. These teams can include well over a dozen members. Foreign negotiators should do as much as they can to avoid being underrepresented.

Learn How to Use Interpreters

The Chinese language is made up of and reflects all the elements of Chinese culture, the intellectual ones as well as the emotional. This makes communication between Westerners and Chinese very difficult, especially when the two sides have to depend on interpreters.

Chinese is an extremely difficult language to interpret or translate with results even 90 percent culturally correct, much less 98 or 99 percent. English is certainly not nearly as difficult to translate verbatim as Chinese is, but its cultural nuances can be totally lost on the Chinese if the interpreter is not knowledgeable and skillful enough to bridge the cultural gaps.

People who have not used interpreters before in a professional situation generally underestimate how difficult it is to correctly interpret both words and cultural nuances so that their meanings are clear. They also underestimate how much trouble can result from interpretations that are off by only one or two percent.

It therefore behooves foreign negotiators to make sure they have an interpreter on hand who has been carefully qualified in advance— not only in his or her understanding of cultural differences, but also in the technical and trade jargon that is part of the presentation.

It goes without saying that use of slang or idioms should be avoided. Also, when a member of the foreign side is talking to one of the Chinese representatives, he or she should look directly at the individual they are addressing—not at the interpreter!

It also helps to have a team member who understands Chinese but keeps it a secret, a team member who has had experience negotiating in China, or a trusted consultant who can send in signals and advice during the game.

Bring Your Own Interpreters

Many Westerners allow their Chinese counterparts to provide the necessary interpreters, a circumstance that can be a serious detriment to the Western side. In such cases, the interpreters naturally tend to first protect their own faces and then the faces of their Chinese employers.

Just as critical in many cases is that interpreters who are Chinese nationals born and educated in China are often not sufficiently grounded in the cultures of the West to accurately translate all of the nuances of English or other Western languages.

Given these circumstances, it is a good idea for Westerners to employ their own interpreters, making sure that they have had extensive cultural experience in both the West and in China, as well as experience in the specific areas of the business concerned.

Leave Lawyers Out

More and more Westerners going into business in China—or already in business there—are bringing lawyers into the mix. This has resulted in the number of lawyers in China growing exponentially.

This is understandable because of the dramatic increase in the legalities involved, but one still hears a chorus of voices saying that it is a mistake for foreign negotiators to have lawyers on their teams from the beginning.

Lawyers are still a recent phenomenon in China, and the last thing most Chinese businesspeople want is to get involved with the law. Because laws are not impartial in China, any legal judgment will not necessarily be based on law.

In fact, companies that have failed in China often got into trouble because they tried litigation after intelligence and strategic failures. When that didn't work their only recourse to be allowed to stay in China was to abjectly apologize to all involved in their area of business and give up options and technology.

The preferred strategy, it seems, is only to bring attorneys in at or near the end of negotiations to make sure everything conforms to the laws that do exist.

Pay Attention to Small Details

Americans and other Westerners are culturally programmed to pay careful attention to big details and less attention to small ones—or to gloss over them entirely. This is not the case in China. The holistic way in which the Chinese think prompts them to pay even more attention to small details than big ones. Proverbs or idioms that teach this principle are a part of the common Chinese culture.

This seemingly small cultural difference has caused inexperienced Western businesspeople more grief—and more delays and loss of money—than can be imagined. The obvious lesson to be learned is that every "i" must be dotted and every "t" crossed in agreements with the Chinese.

When small details are not spelled out clearly and completely from the beginning in their business relationships, the Chinese automatically interpret things the way they see fit. This invariably causes problems because the foreign side does not like the results.

Beware of Using Humor

Consultants are forever warning Western businesspeople away from using humor in their speeches and presentations in China. Attempts at humor likely wouldn't be understood and could have a negative rather than positive effect.

This is not to say that a sense of humor is lacking in the Chinese; they appreciate humor just as much as people of any other culture. The problem here is that Western humor often does not communicate through the cultural and language differences involved. Before using humor in front of a Chinese negotiating team or audience, it is wise to have it culture-tested in advance.

Dress the Part

Traditional emphasis on the importance of dressing conservatively in China is passé. There is no specific Chinese custom for business attire. While the overall standard of dress may be more conservative than what would be expected in Los Angeles, for example, the standards that prevail in London, New York, Paris, Tokyo, and other international cities are perfectly acceptable in China.

This said, business attire should still be relatively conservative and unpretentious. Bright colors should be avoided. Women should wear conservative business suits or dresses with high necklines and flat shoes or ones with low heels.

Chapter 10

What to Expect While Negotiating

Meeting protocol in China is generally more formal than in the United States, but it is comparable to that of European and Latin cultures.

It is worth noting that the Chinese attempt to control every aspect of meetings, from greetings and introductions to the order of seating, the content of the discussions, and how they are conducted. This is not entirely a ploy to take and keep the advantage, although that is surely a primary aim. It is also to ensure that the meeting goes smoothly and that there are no surprises.

The senior person on each team normally will enter the meeting room first, a practice that clearly identifies the team leaders. Once all the team members are in the room the Chinese side will prepare for introductions by loosely lining up in order of rank, with the senior person in the middle of the line. The foreign side should, of course, do the same.

If the leader of the Chinese team speaks even a small amount of English he or she will generally step forward and introduce him- or herself. If the leader of the foreign team knows enough Chinese to make a self-introduction, doing so is a good step forward.

Otherwise a bilingual individual on the Chinese side will usually handle introductions, beginning with the two team leaders.

As soon as the team leaders have been introduced, the rest of the lineup on each side follows suit. At this point, team members step out of line to introduce themselves to the people who are not opposite of them, resulting in both teams milling around until everyone has met.

While introducing themselves, individuals shake hands and then exchange business cards. This is an excellent opportunity for foreign visitors to greet their counterparts in both English and Chinese, even if all they can say in Chinese is *Hen gaoxing renshi ni* (hen ga-oh-sheeng ren-shu nee)—"I'm pleased to meet you!"

The correct method of exchanging business cards in China is often discussed. The old advice that you should present your card with both hands and accept the other person's card in the way is just that—old advice. Some Chinese do; some don't. It depends on their level of internationalization. In short, if they use both hands, you should, too. (If you do and they don't, it makes you look out-of-date.)

For the Chinese, the first meeting is primarily a get-acquainted event and it is common for the two teams to mingle and chat for several minutes before taking their places at the meeting table. This is typically followed by introductory welcoming remarks from the Chinese team leader or leaders, followed by suitable comments from the spokespersons for the foreign side.

The Chinese side will then invite the foreign side to make a preliminary presentation covering the highlights of their proposal. All too often, however, the foreign team will make its full presentation, with Americans in particular laying everything out in detail. This gives the Chinese an advantage from the start by allowing them to ask a lengthy series of questions and tailor their own position as the proceedings progress.

Leaders of Chinese negotiating teams will act as spokespersons for the whole group. Generally, individual team members won't speak up unless asked to do so by their leader. Whatever differences of opinion the members of the Chinese group may have are resolved before or after the meeting. American customs allowing anyone to speak out during meetings and the hashing out of differences on the spot goes against the Chinese grain.

Westerners should also be aware that how you spend your time after the meeting is a factor key for successful negotiations. Because the Chinese way of negotiating can be counterintuitive for Westerners, these after-hours meetings can give them a good opportunity to discover how the negotiations are proceeding.

If the Chinese team does not arrange for a meeting at a bar or other entertainment facility (or a day tour they insist that the foreigners take, and so on), the foreign side should extend an invitation to the whole Chinese team without putting any individual on the spot.

Ideally, the key figures in the group will show up. If they don't attend and offer no explanation why, it can be an indication that things are not going well.

The Business Card Imperative

It is very important for visiting foreign businesspeople to have an ample supply of name cards, preferably well-designed ones printed on attractive paper stock. These cards in effect represent their owner's face.

It is also important to have business cards printed in your native language on one side and in Chinese on the other using the simplified characters used for Mandarin.

After the members of the foreign team sit down at the meeting table they should arrange the cards they received from their Chinese counterparts on the table in front of them in the order in which the Chinese are seated on the opposite side of the table. This will help them to identify the various individuals during the meeting.

It is wise to make sure the order of the cards is correct. If you are not sure, hold up the card in question and call out the name on it; the card's owner will identify him- or herself. This process may take two or three minutes to accomplish as each member shuffles his or her cards around, but it is an important step and should be done.

Addressing the Senior Person

During negotiations and other group contact with the Chinese it is especially important for Western businesspeople to know the rank of the individuals involved. Comments should be addressed to the most senior person unless they are in response to a question or remark from someone of lower rank.

During negotiating sessions this may not be as simple as it sounds, because it is not uncommon for senior members of the Chinese side to sit among its lower ranking members and remain quiet. These individuals may not introduce themselves or may have name cards with innocuous titles that do not reveal their positions. There is no quick solution to this situation, so the only recourse for the foreign side is to address the person who is acting as the team's leader, while keeping in mind that he or she may not be the highest ranking person in the room.

Sit Up Straight & Stand Tall!

Western businesspeople should not be surprised to hear that the ways they sit and stand when engaged in formal business discussions with the Chinese are important. Most Westerners know the difference between slouching and sitting or standing in a formal or semiformal manner, and they should be conscious of their posture in business situations.

The fact is, Chinese etiquette is not that different from formal etiquette in most European countries—or even refined kinds of etiquette that still exist in the United States. The difference, however, is that the Chinese are more formal and ritualistic in their day-to-day behavior than Americans and some other Westerners.

Informal behavior during business meetings and in other situations the Chinese regard to be formal is seen as a sign of insincerity and lack of respect for the purpose of the meeting and the people involved in it.

There is a time for relaxing and behaving informally in the world of Chinese business, but it is not during meetings. Instead this should be reserved for after-hours meetings in places like bars, cabarets, and restaurants.

During negotiation sessions and other meetings with the Chinese a relatively high degree of formal protocol is important. Because doing business in China is a personal thing, however, friendly but restrained levity before and after meetings is very much in order.

Keep a Damper on Your Enthusiasm

It is natural for a foreign negotiating team going to China to behave in an enthusiastic manner. At certain times during the negotiation process enthusiasm can be a plus, but a high level of it throughout the entire process strikes the Chinese as overly aggressive and impolite.

Well-timed enthusiasm should be shown now and then between periods of quiet, harmonious behavior.

Make a Series of Short Presentations

The Chinese do not like long presentations. They prefer relatively brief discussions of points of interest, especially ones addressing how things will be done, and generally are not concerned that these points be covered in a particular order.

When foreign negotiators make long presentations it is common for the attention of the Chinese to wander, and after a certain point they simply stop listening.

The obvious response is for foreign negotiators to break their long presentations into several shorter parts, asking for comments and questions after each one.

Keep Notes at Meetings

The Chinese always have at least one bilingual individual on their team whose sole purpose is to take notes of everything that is said. Note taking is just common sense, but foreigners will occasionally fail to do so. Whether this oversight happens because of the language barrier or because the Western team has their agenda written down in precise detail, they will almost always end up regretting it.

Confirm Mutual Understanding
& Summarize the Meeting

Throughout the course of negotiations with the Chinese it pays to confirm the understanding of both parties on a step-by-step basis, rather than after a long series of steps. This allows foreigners to keep better track of what has happened and have a much better chance of recognizing when they are nearing the end of negotiation. Otherwise, there is no way to check the progress.

Another obvious piece of advice is that the final act at the end of daily meetings should be a summary of what was discussed and agreed on.

Ask the Right Questions

Foreign negotiators should craft in advance an extensive series of questions to ask their Chinese counterparts and add to the list during meetings. The Chinese are notorious for the number of questions they ask. In contrast, Westerners are known for being reluctant to ask questions of Asian businesspeople and government officials, because they don't want to appear to be too aggressive or to irritate the other side.

It is not easy to come up with the right questions and ask them in the right way, but doing so is an essential element in arriving at mutual understanding. Questions should not be asked in an accusing or antagonizing tone, and it can be important to phrase them in what may seem to be an indirect manner. The Chinese can react negatively to being questioned too directly, so it is often necessary to ask many questions before a clear answer emerges.

Striking Like a Snake

The Chinese techniques of negotiation have been likened to both guerrilla and psychological warfare. Their strategies often follow a pattern appropriate for the battlefield—strike, retreat; strike, retreat; confuse the enemy; get them off guard; weaken their will; make them feel guilty for opposing you; and then make a "final offer" that is considerably below what they know is acceptable.

This strike-retreat technique apparently springs from the same principle as the martial art *dai ji juan* (die jee jwahn), which is said to have been created by a priest after watching a bird of prey attack a snake. In its attempt to strike the snake, the bird eventually wore itself down, made a mistake, and was nailed by the writhing reptile. The thrashing of opponents as they simultaneously try to defend themselves and mount a counterattack can be likened to this struggle.

Unlike most foreign businesspeople, Chinese officials and managers have often had considerable experience in using psychological tactics in cross-examining and intimidating opponents.

Withholding Information

Another tactic in the Chinese way of negotiation is to withhold information important to the discussions, commonly including the government's position and how it will affect any agreement. The foreign team's only recourse is to be aware of this tactic and do as the Chinese do: continuously ask questions, even the same ones worded differently, until the situation is as clear as possible.

Although the Chinese tend to spring surprises on both enemies and possible business partners, they themselves are seriously upset when the tables are turned. This should be taken into consideration in any dealings with the Chinese, and the possibility of negative fall-out weighed carefully.

The "Hit-Run" Tactic

Another approach commonly used by Chinese negotiators has been described as a "hit-run" tactic, meaning they will "hit" the foreign team with something that is unexpected and upsetting, and then back off if the response from the foreign side is shock and dismay.

The best way to diffuse this tactic is remaining calm and asking a lot of questions that eventually demolish the problem.

The Passive Face Ploy

Newcomers to China should not be put off by the lack of animation among their Chinese counterparts during formal discussions. Nonverbal communication in such settings speaks volumes.

The Chinese have been conditioned to maintain passive facial expressions during formal meetings. They may also close their eyes or not focus them on the speaker. These practices are designed to maintain harmony during the meeting, avoid influencing the speaker, and most important avoid giving away their feelings.

They have also learned to use these traditional cultural practices to their advantage when negotiating with foreigners. This upsets foreigners, who take it to mean they are not getting through, get flustered, repeat themselves, talk louder, and otherwise lose their aplomb. This obviously gives the Chinese negotiators a considerable advantage.

Silence as a Negotiating Tactic

From the days of Confucius and Lao Tzu the Chinese were advised that it was better (and safer) to stay silent than to speak. This eventually became such a key part of Chinese etiquette that being talkative was regarded as impolite and big talkers were believed to be insincere and untrustworthy.

This attitude is still found in present-day China and should be kept in mind by businesspeople. It is normal for Chinese negotiators to let the foreign side talk and remain silent except when asking questions—a technique that has been referred to as killing with silence, since it "kills" the spirit of the opposing team.

The Chinese are masters at using silence when negotiating with Americans and other Westerners. Americans, in particular, do not know how to handle silence during a meeting. They tend to become concerned that something is wrong and grow increasingly impatient and flustered.

In addition, there is a pronounced tendency for those who are not experienced in cross-cultural communication to automatically assume that the more they talk the more likely they are to get their points across. This tendency is often kicked into high gear when foreign businesspeople are making presentations in China, Japan, Korea, or elsewhere in the Confucian sphere of Asia.

As Western negotiators talk to fill the silence, it is common for them to repeat themselves a number of times and gradually weaken their position. A better response is for the Western team to stop presenting, talk quietly and privately among themselves, get a drink, go to the restroom, and so on. When the Chinese side sees that the Westerners are not flustered and won't break down, they will usually signal they are ready to continue the meeting.

What to Do When They Leave the Room?

Foreigners who have not had any negotiating experience in China are often surprised and upset when a member of the other team gets up and leaves the room without any explanation.

Because the Chinese do not see negotiating sessions as progressing from A to Z in a straight line, they are not concerned with missing anything. To them, the process of negotiation is a circle allowing discussion to start anywhere and cover any topic at any time. Furthermore, it is possible to miss chunks of the negotiations because the Chinese side will eventually ask questions over and over from different angles until everything finally becomes clear.

The only choice you have in this situation is to continue answering all the questions that are posed and come up with as many questions of your own as you can. You should not take it as a slight when someone leaves the meeting, or let it break your train of thought. Just go on as if it never happened.

The Intimidation & Anger Tactics

Foreigners who have never negotiated with the Chinese are typically surprised when one or more of their counterparts suddenly takes an aggressive stance and begins saying things designed to intimidate them. This may take the form of an angry outburst using language and movements dramatically different from the normally harmonious behavior of the Chinese.

Westerners should keep in mind that this behavior is simply part of the traditional style of negotiation in China. This is guided by Sun Tzu's *The Art of War*, which encourages leaders to do everything possible to demoralize the enemy

As frustrating as it can be to Westerners who have been conditioned to take a fundamentally different approach to business negotiations, such displays of anger should not be taken personally or allowed to derail their fact-based, logical, rational, and professional approach to achieving an equitable agreement.

It is important for foreigners engaging in business discussions in China to keep their own emotions under control and avoid showing any signs of anger. Loosing your temper, confronting someone, putting someone on the spot, behaving arrogantly, or failing to accord proper respect can cause a serious loss of face, and is likely to end the negotiations. This has happened in the past, and resulted in the foreign side having to bring in a high-ranking third party to smooth things over, apologize profusely, and humble themselves to get the negotiations back on track.

Using Competitors as Bogeymen

Another common ploy used by Chinese negotiators is to claim that a competitor is waiting to jump in if you don't accept their terms. This may or may not be true, so some sleuthing might be in order. In any event, Western businesspeople should be firm enough in their goals and requirements to walk away if the terms offered are not suitable.

In fact, some Chinese companies have indeed been known to conduct parallel negotiations with a competitor to get more intelligence that they can use.

Compromising the Right Way

Compromising is an essential part of business negotiations. However, problems often arise during negotiations because the Western side reveals its hand too early in the game.

This is sometimes caused by the guerrilla tactics of the Chinese, which can upset the equilibrium of inexperienced Western negotiators so much that they will reveal outright how much they are willing to compromise their first offer, or hint broadly that they are, of course, prepared to compromise their position.

Even when the Chinese concerned have no experience in negotiating with Westerners, they recognize an advantage when they see one. The common response to admissions like these is to say that since the foreign side's position is flexible, the apparently stalled negotiations can be restarted after the compromises have been made.

To counter this approach the Western side must be able and willing to invest time (and money) in the negotiating process. One tactic that often works is repeatedly asking the Chinese side questions about how serious they are, how badly they want to make a deal, and how far they are prepared to go. This can go on for hours, days, weeks, or even longer, but when the Chinese see that the foreign side is not going to cave in, they will usually begin to move forward small step by small step.

One way of keeping the Chinese side in a positive mood is to say and do things that give face to the individuals, their companies, and China. Favorable or complimentary comments or acts make negotiators feel good, showing that you are a "friend" of China and are there to make a contribution, not just a profit.

Authority Levels Matter

One thing to keep in mind while negotiating is that the Chinese team generally cannot make binding decisions at the table. They usually have to get clearance and a consensus approval from a number of people in their own companies as well as a number of government officials.

While foreign businesspeople on a high executive level usually have the authority to make decisions on the spot and make changes in company policy—or at least what the company will accept in a particular situation—the Chinese either do not have such authority or will claim that they don't when it suits their purpose.

As in other facets of Chinese culture, there is also little feeling of individual responsibility in negotiations. Relationships in Chinese business are not between people, but rather between bureaucratic organizations, and therefore are conducted on a higher, abstract level. This worldview means that the individual Chinese businessperson or government official can never be pinned down personally. He or she always has an out and can delay or stop negotiations with personal impunity, all in the name of their organization.

Using Go-betweens

Several cultural factors result in the Chinese routinely using *zhongjian ren* (johng-jee-in ren), or go-betweens, in their business and social relationships. The first is the Chinese predisposition to divide people into two groups—an inner circle of family and friends versus outsiders or strangers. Because these outsiders have no obligation to help them, the Chinese tend to avoid direct contact with people outside this inner circle.

Another factor is the extraordinary Chinese concern with face— their own and that of others. The possibility of losing face as a result of direct contact with a stranger increases their tendency to avoid contact with people they don't know. The Chinese are especially reluctant to personally give bad news to anyone, and the fear of failure or rejection weighs heavily on them.

This makes the Chinese reluctant to speak frankly or clearly to people directly involved in many situations, especially about matters that might reflect badly on them or that involve others. Instead of doing so, they make significant use of go-betweens. These go-betweens are often people with whom they have good *guanxi*—in other words, people who owe them favors.

Foreign businesspeople in China are likely to find the tactic of using go-betweens to be invaluable. They often have no choice but to use them in their relations with government agencies and other enterprises, in particular, because they themselves cannot get straight answers or the progress they need.

Some companies have learned that the Chinese are just as impressed with celebrities as Americans and others, and have enlisted as go-betweens internationally known diplomats, ex-politicians, former presidents, and others to jump-start their personal relationships in China.

When negotiations are not making any progress, or seem on the verge of breaking down altogether, it can be very helpful to engage a go-between to act as liaison with the Chinese company. The Chinese will generally reveal to a trusted third party what they are really thinking—and what they really want.

Keep on Negotiating!

One of the most common complaints that Westerners have about their relationships with Chinese is that the Chinese never stop negotiating. Even after contracts are signed, the Chinese side invariably continues asking questions, requesting more information, or seeking changes to the contract.

Western businesspeople should be prepared for ongoing dialogue with their Chinese counterparts and regard it as a normal part of doing business in China. This requires keeping the lines of communication open at all times, monitoring joint activities, solving problems as they occur, and making adjustments in the relationship as needed.

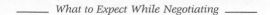

This means the Western side must assign people to the task who are capable of functioning efficiently in this environment, and who have direct access to top management around the clock.

Chapter 11

Business Entertainment

Business entertainment is a major industry in China. To avoid the strict ritualistic etiquette required in formal occasions by Chinese culture, the practical Chinese quickly developed an auxiliary route to getting to know one another, hashing out the details of alliances and deals, and so on. Rather than limiting business dealings to the office and corporate conference rooms, the Chinese made dining and drinking together an integral part of the process.

Because drinking alcoholic beverages lowers inhibitions and allows people to say and do things not allowed by the rules of etiquette, drinking became the primary facilitator of genuine, unfettered human relations in China. And because eating together is one of the fundamental elements in familial relationships, banquet-style meals became a staple of business, political, and other professional relations in China, much as in the rest of the world. Banquet-style dinners are one of the leading venues for coming to terms on contracts and building and sustaining the all-important personal relationships that are the foundation of business in China.

Other popular entertainment venues include bars and clubs where drinking and karaoke-style singing sessions are held—so you may want to practice singing a couple of popular songs in advance. The investment of time and effort will pay off.

In addition, the Western custom of holding business breakfasts and lunches has become common in China. In fact, "morning tea" has been a popular business custom in Fujian and Guangdong provinces for a long time. Taking the initiative and inviting Chinese contacts to these meetings is an excellent way to avoid the pressure to drink and the obligation to spend time in bars or other places after working hours.

If luncheon and breakfast meetings are semiformal, taking place in a private room of a restaurant or hotel or a special section of a restaurant, the protocol relating to the seating of senior members and ranking guests is observed. Generally, the host sits in the seat in the middle of the table facing the door. The ranking guest sits on the host's right side and the next in rank sits to his or her left. If interpreters are being used, they sit next to the ranking guests.

The more formal the meeting, the more likely the host will make a few remarks and call for a *ganbei* (gan-bay), or "bottoms up," toast after several minutes of chatting. The senior guest usually responds with suitable comments, followed by another *ganbei* toast, all done in a friendly informal manner.

In China dining and drinking together to facilitate professional relationships is more common, more formal, and plays a much more important role than in the rest of the world. Meetings away from professional settings are often actually more important than ones that take place on company or government premises because they are less formal and the exchange of information, opinions, and positions is often more extensive.

Business & Official Banquets

China is famous for banquets that are staged for foreign political dignitaries and these well-publicized events have made the word Moutai (moh-tie), the official drink of such banquets, known around the world.

Although similar banquets are commonly held in the United States, Europe, and other places around the world, it certainly seems that there are more business banquets held in China than in other countries. These affairs generally follow a well-established protocol, although the etiquette is not really as strict as it would be at a royal bash, for example.

Business banquets for foreign visitors are often held at restaurants inside international hotels. In most cases, hosts and guests arrive before the table or tables are set, and will mill around in an outer room chatting together.

When the signal is given to enter the dining room, the traditional ritual is for guests and hosts to enter according to their rank, with the host accompanying the ranking guest. Seating is based around the host and ranking guest taking the power positions at the table. They sit next to each other at what is understood to be the head of the table, the side facing the door with a wall or window behind it.

Once seated, the hosts typically applaud the guests. It is proper etiquette for the guests to applaud at the same time.

At the beginning of smaller banquets, the host may make a show of serving the senior guest or guests, but after everyone starts eating guests serve themselves. Guests are invariably told to try every dish to avoid insulting the host, but that is a quaint bit of advice. After the first few courses when everyone is busy eating and talking, nobody is keeping score. You can safely go light or heavy on individual courses or skip some altogether.

It is wise to give your banquet's host face by commenting on the dishes that you really like during the meal and thanking him or her. Another common courtesy that isn't unique to China is commenting on how delicious the whole meal has been when it is drawing to a close.

Reciprocal Banquet Hosting

Foreign business groups that have been treated to a banquet by their Chinese hosts should reciprocate with a comparable banquet near the end of their trips. Restaurants in Western-style hotels are acceptable for this purpose.

Because banquets are very involved, the event should be planned in advance with the hotel catering manager.

When extending invitations to a banquet, be specific. The Chinese can be more literal and may take at face value vague intentions like "next week."

Discreet inquiries should be made to your primary liaison to discover if the Chinese side would like to have, or agree to, a Western meal rather than a Chinese one. If the meal is to be Chinese, special attention should be paid to the menu and the order in which the dishes are served, as required by the yin-yang principle.

When hosting a banquet, a senior member of the Western group should arrive early to attend to the details, especially seating arrangements that indicate the rank and status of the guests.

When entertaining at Western hotels long rectangular tables can be used instead of China's traditional round ones, even when the meal is to be Chinese. But psychologically speaking, round tables are far more powerful than square or rectangular tables, enhancing friendly feelings and intimate conversations—something the Chinese learned a long time ago.

Alcohol & Business

In China it is believed that you cannot really get to know a person until enough alcohol is imbibed to cause him or her to disregard etiquette and behave in a natural way. This is a primary reason why drinking is an integral part of both social and business relationships in China, and why Chinese hosts typically encourage new foreign contacts to drink. (Drivers and interpreters are normally excused from the pressure to drink.)

However businesspeople and other visitors to China should keep in mind that the Chinese did not traditionally mix eating and the drinking of alcoholic beverages; they drink before starting to eat. This is still the general rule, but more and more people now continue to drink, especially beer, after they start eating. Many Chinese people like to click glasses when they toast. However, this is impractical for people sitting around a banquet table, so instead they lift their glasses in the air, as people do elsewhere when toasting a number of people. Alternately, it has become a habit in many areas of China for people to tap their glasses on the round countertop of the lazy Susan as a substitute for clicking glasses during a toast.

There is often considerable pressure on foreigners to join in on the drinking. This can be a problem for those who don't drink or who do so only moderately because refusing to drink may put the Chinese in an awkward and potentially embarrassing position, particularly at after-hours dinners and at karaoke bars.

Without presenting a plausible excuse for refusing alcoholic drinks, guests lose face and also cause their hosts to lose face. A medical condition is acceptable as a reason for not drinking. Saying in advance that you are allergic to alcohol is only partially acceptable. Some Chinese people are extraordinarily susceptible to alcohol, becoming beet red and getting sick after only a few sips, but that doesn't stop many of them from drinking.

At evening banquets an endless round of toasts often results in some participants getting drunk. If your Chinese counterparts drink and get tipsy and you don't, it puts a damper on the party atmosphere. My own solution is to drink very moderately and put on an act to avoid spoiling the party. If you can't or won't drink, you should advise your Chinese counterparts in advance—no matter who is hosting the outing—so you can have a different kind of event.

While there is no protocol for drinking during luncheon meetings it is common enough for the participants to order beer and toast each other, but there is no pressure on you to drink to drunkenness. On these occasions, it is perfectly all right to order juice or some other nonalcoholic drink and use it to participate in the toasts. This, of course, is an occasion for visitors to use their knowledge of Chinese by joining on the *ganbei* toast.

At daytime business banquets hosted by the Chinese, you can avoid embarrassing anyone by informing your host in advance that you are able to drink only nonalcoholic beverages.

Answering Personal Questions

Foreigners in China shouldn't be put off by questions more personal than what they are used to. It is part of Chinese etiquette to ask personal questions to determine the social and economic statuses of the people they meet. Proper behavior is based on hierarchy and rank, and the people asking the questions want to know how to treat you.

In work situations, some Chinese may ask foreign employees about their salaries and benefits. This is not always related to proper etiquette. It may be because they want to know how much wage discrimination there is between Chinese and foreign employees. The only recourse to this is to respond that management level wages are regarded by the company as confidential.

Gift Giving Is Dangerous

In response to multiple scandals and to put a stop to the rampant corruption that characterizes Chinese government and business, the Chinese government has labeled gift giving as bribery, with the exception of small gifts given as a token. However, even though tens of thousands of people have been swept up in government bribery investigations, gift-giving is still very much a part of Chinese life.

Despite the volume of etiquette advice on how and what to give as gifts in new travel books and old business guides, foreign businesspeople should not get caught up in this mess. Government officials are prohibited from accepting any gifts whatsoever, and the more internationalized companies also have rules against it.

When normal gift-giving situations arise among business contacts—such as a promotion, the birth of a child, and so on—it is perfectly acceptable to give appropriate gifts privately as personal gestures.

Gift giving by companies to suppliers and clients on auspicious occasions such as New Year's has long been a tradition in China, and is both legitimate and legal. However, there are restrictions on what can be given and its value. Experienced lawyers and others say this kind of gift giving is not worth the risk, and advise against it.

Patrick Norton, a lawyer at O'Melveny & Myers in Washington, D.C., and an expert on China's Foreign Corrupt Practices Act, says where gifts to government officials are concerned, some promotional activities may be allowed, but "the operative language in the statute is you can't provide a government official anything of value."

It has also been pointed out, however, that even a valuable gift does not constitute bribery if the recipient did not promise to do something for it. However, the Chinese government will almost certainly not accept this as a defense.

Chapter 12

When You Are Host in Your Own Country

A great deal has been written about hosting Chinese delegations visiting your own country. All kinds of advice is given, most of which is unnecessary and some of which is rather ludicrous.

The Chinese who travel abroad for business purposes do not expect to be met with Chinese etiquette. They do not expect their hosts to mimic typical or traditional Chinese behavior. The Chinese are not so frozen in their own culture that they cannot respond to and appreciate the customs of other people. They want to see and experience the behavior and customs of the country they are in!

This does not, of course, mean they can or should be subjected to coarse behavior. It does mean that what is regarded to be good behavior in the host country is certainly good enough for visitors from abroad, including behavior-conscious Chinese.

When hosting a delegation from China, it goes without saying that you should greet them at the airport, escort them to their hotel, provide them with a schedule of meetings and other activities, and be willing to respond to any requests they may have. The senior member of the welcoming committee should be close in rank to the senior individual in the Chinese group. A president, for example, can be met by a senior vice president.

Visitors shouldn't be taken to a Chinese restaurant unless they specifically ask to be. Early in the visit you should invite them to your home for dinner. Home invitations are still relatively rare in China, so it can be something special for them to see how people in your country live. In this case, they should be treated in exactly the same way you would treat any valued guest.

Whatever the purpose of the meeting, you should follow the normal legal and moral procedures that are desirable in any business relationship. The same customs regarding introductions, seating, chatting before a meeting is called to order, and so on, that apply to formal meetings in your own company can be followed without worry.

This said, you must still deal with cultural differences and the official rules and requirements the Chinese group must contend with. You will have to be persistent but diplomatic, exercise extraordinary patience, and keep in mind that signing a contract does not mean the deal is done, just as if you were in China.

However, the traditional Chinese way of doing business is often neither practical nor rational by Western standards, and it makes no sense for people from other countries to follow any Chinese business practices that are disadvantageous and limiting to both parties when not in China.

Getting Personal

The visitors should not be rushed into any kind of program on the day they arrive, especially if they arrive in the late afternoon. If they request some kind of activity, however, they should be accommodated.

On the first full day, time should be allocated for the members of both teams to get to know one another. This can be done in number of ways, including a personal dinner, a tour through a factory, a sightseeing tour, or a combination of such things.

Structuring the Meeting Room

Generally, nothing special must be done to accommodate Chinese guests at formal business meetings. The Chinese should be seated at what is considered the head of the table, so that they face the door with their backs to any windows. Regardless of the room's setup, the head of table should be obvious (even without training in feng shui).

Any pertinent materials that the Chinese have not already received should be on the table, along with a packet of information about the local city.

Providing Refreshments

A lower-ranking member of your team should be charged with the responsibility of asking his or her equivalent on the Chinese team in advance if there are any special requests for refreshments. Otherwise, a choice of coffee, tea, one or two kinds of fruit juice, and water should be available.

Preliminary Remarks

The senior person on the foreign team should make some welcoming remarks and comments, thanking the Chinese for making the long trip from China and briefly stating what they hope to accomplish during the meetings.

This opening, which should not be hurried, should also be used as an opportunity to reintroduce all of the members of your team. Profiles should be given of their educational backgrounds and work experiences, information that should also have been sent to China in advance, allowing the Chinese to connect the information with the face of the individual.

Giving Your Guests Face

You should make a point of acknowledging the amazing economic and social progress that China has made since the 1980s, noting that you are delighted to see that China has regained its position as the Middle Kingdom and has become a world leader. You should also have done enough research on the company or organization you are hosting to make equally complimentary comments about it, referring to specific things.

Inviting Guests Out for the Evening

If the senior person in your group has not already entertained the guests at his or her home, the first evening after meetings begin is the time to do so. The ideal fare at such private dinners is whatever the area is locally famous for—cowboy-style steak cookouts, backyard barbecues, sit-down dinners featuring local specialties, and so on.

Guests also expect to sample the local nightlife, which can be arranged for the third or fourth night of their stay. This generally refers to cabarets or nightclubs where there is entertainment. If there are women in the group these settings should not include places where they might feel uncomfortable.

Paying Bills

Whether at home or abroad, the Chinese will often attempt to pay bar or nightclub bills when they are invited out by foreign hosts. This is a tried and proven way of developing social credit with people, especially unwary foreigners.

The foreign host should make a specific point of paying the bill before the evening ends. As in China, you might consider making arrangements in advance for the bill to be surreptitiously delivered to you or to be called away from the party so you can pay it.

Seeing Your Guests Off

Your Chinese guests will probably want to host you for a farewell dinner party, and you will usually be informed in advance. If not, it will come up if you announce that you have an evening planned. The end of the farewell dinner is a good time to present your guests with gifts for themselves, their spouses, and their children, allowing time for them to be packed away before the group leaves the next day.

The foreign host should designate a small delegation to see the Chinese guests off at the local airport, again keeping in mind that rank counts and that you gain and give face by adhering to this particular protocol.

Appendix

Selected Vocabulary &
Useful Expressions

Although there are a number of languages and many regional dialects spoken in different parts of China, the national language is Mandarin. It is perfectly all right for you to use Mandarin wherever you are in China.

The Chinese appreciate it when foreign visitors speak—or try to speak—to them in their language, and are tolerant of faulty attempts because they are well aware that it is difficult for foreigners to quickly master the up-and-down tones of the language.

I have included English-language phonetics for the Chinese words and phrases used in this book. They do not account for the tones, but they are generally close enough that you will be understood. Here are personal titles, some common greetings, and useful expressions.

Personal Titles

Mr *Xiansheng* (she-inn-shuung)

Miss *Xiaojie* (she-ow-jay)

Ms *Nushi* (nu-she)

Madame or Mrs *Furen* (fuu-wren) or *Taitai* (tie-tie)

Master *Shifu* (shurr-fuu)—This term of respect is used to address professional people whose names you do not know, including waiters, chefs, craftsmen, repairmen, and so on.

Family Relationships

Family *Jiá* (jee-ah)

Family name *Jiá Xingming* (jee-ah sheeng-meeng)

Given name *Mingzi* (meeng-dzu)

Father *Fúqin* (fuuu-cheen)

Mother *Mǔqin* (muuu-cheen)

Husband *Zhángfu* (jahng-fuu)

Wife *Qizi* (chee-zu)

Wife, madame *Taitai* (tie-tie)

Children *Háizi* (hie-zu)

Age *Niánling* (nee-enn leeng)

Oldest child *Laoda* (lough-dah)

Second-born child *Lao'er* (lough-urr)

Third-born child *Laosan* (louth-sahn)

Youngest child *Laoyao* (lough-yow)

Elder brother *Xiong* (she-ohng)

Youngest brother *Xiaodi* (she-ow-dee)

Corporate Titles

Chairman of the Board *Dongshizhang* (doong-she-jahng)

President *Zongcai* (johng-t'sie)

Managing Director *Zhong jingli* (johng jeeng-lee)

Manager *Jingli* (jeeng-lee)

Head of a factory *Changzhang* (chahng-jahng)

Government Titles

Minister *Buzhang* (buu-jahng)

Bureau Director *Juzhang* (juu-jahng)

Division Director *Chuzhang* (chuu-jahng)

Governor *Shengzhang* (shuung-jahng)

Mayor *Shizhang* (she-jahng)

Everyday Expressions

Hello *Ni hao* (Nee how)—*Ni hao* is also used as the equivalent of good morning, good afternoon, and good evening, but there are also specific terms for these expressions. It is also the form of greeting that is used by Chinese to foreigners, and is also recommended for foreigners to use to Chinese.

Hello (said to an older person) *Nin hao* (Neen-how)—This is a more polite form of *ni hao,* commonly used when speaking to seniors.

You may hear the Chinese use a variety of greetings among themselves. Here are some of the most common:

Chiguo fan le? (Chuh-gwaw fahn luh?)
Have you eaten?—This traditional greeting is becoming less common, especially in the developed areas of China, as there is less concern about the next meal.

Mang ma? (Mahng mah?)
Are you busy?—This is now a common greeting among Chinese, particularly among friends. It is the equivalent of "What's up?" and "How are you doing?"

Nin qu nar a? (Neen chu nahhr ah?)
Where are you going?—This is more or less the equivalent of "What are you up to?"

Other expressions that are used as greetings include references to things people are doing, such as "You are reading," "You are working," and so on.

Useful Sentences

Saying Hello and Good-bye

Good morning (until about 10 a.m.) *Zaoshang hao* (Zow-shahng how)

Good afternoon *Xiawu hao* (Shee-ah-woo how)

Good evening *Wanshang hao* (Wahn-shahng how)

Good night *Wan an* (Wahn ahn)

Hello, manager *Jingli hao* (Jeeng-lee how)—It is common in China to greet people by their titles. *Jingli* (jeeng-lee) means "manager," so *jingli hao* is the equivalent of hello, good morning, good afternoon, or good evening, manager; much as a Westerner might say, "Good morning, boss."

Is it time to go? *Jidian zou?* (Jee-dee-in zoe?)

Good-bye *Zai-jian* (Zigh-jee-in)

Excuse me (May I trouble you?) *Mafan ni* (Mah-fahn nee)

Excuse me (to get attention) *Lao jia* (Lough jee-ah)

Getting to Know Each Other

What is your name? *Ni jiao shenme mingzi?*
(Nee jee-ow shuun-muh meeng-dzu?)

My name is_____
Wo jiao _____ (Waw jee-ow_____)

What is your family name?
Ni xing shenme? (Nee sheeng shuhn-muh)

My family name is_____
Wo xing _____ (Waw sheeng_____)

This is Mr _____ *Zhe wei shi* _____ *xiansheng*
(Dze way shuh _____ she-inn-shuung)

This is Mrs _____ *Zhe wei shi* _____ *tu ran*
(Dzu way shuh _____ too wren)

This is Miss _____ *Zhe wei shi* _____ *xiajia*
(Dzu way shuh _____ she-ah-jah)

I'm pleased to meet you
Hen gaoxing renshi ni (Hin gow-sheeng wren-shuh nee)
OR *Jiuyang* (jew-yahng)

I am an American
Wo shi Meiguo ren (Waw shuh May-gwoh wren)

I am a Canadian
Wo shi Jianada ren (Waw shuh Jee-ah-nah-dah wren)

I am British *Wo shi Yingguo ren* (Waw shuh Eeen-gwoh wren)

I am Australian *Wo shi Aodaliya ren*
(Waw shuh Ah-oh-dah-lee-yah wren)

I am on a holiday *Wo lai dujia* (Waw lie duu-jah)

I am here on business
Wo lai zuo shengyi (Waw lie dzwoh shuung-ee)

In Conversation

Thank you *Xie xie* (Shay shay)

Very good *Hen hao* (Hin how)

That's no good *Bu hao* (Boo how)

That's right *Duile* (Dwee-luh)

That's all right *Mei guanxi* (May gwahn-she)

All right/okay *Hao/hao ba* (How/how bah)

Please come in *Qing jin* (Cheeng-jeen)

Please sit down *Qing zuó* (Cheeng dzwoh)

Welcome *Huánying* (Hwahn-eeng)

You are welcome *Bú xié* (Boo shay)

Don't mention it *Bú kéqi* (Boo kuh-chee)

Excuse me/sorry *Dui búqi* (Dwee boo-chee)

I'm sorry/I apologize *Duibuqi* (Dwee-boo-chee)

I am very sorry: *Hen baoqian* (Hin bow-chee-in)

Please hurry!: *Qing gankuai!* (Cheeng gahn-kwie!)

I know: *Wo zhidao* (Waw jr-dow)

I don't know: *Wo bu zhidao* (Waw buu jr-dow)

I understand: *Wo dong* (Waw doong)

I don't understand: *Wo bu dong* (Wa boo doong)

Do you understand? *Dong ma?* (Doong mah?)

Do you speak English?
Ni hui Yingwen ma? (Nee hwee Eeng-wun mah?)

Please repeat that *Qing ni zaishuo yibian*
(Cheeng nee zigh-shwaw ee-bee-in)

What did you say?
Ni shou shenma? (Nee shwaw shen-mah?)

I need an interpreter
Wo xuyao fanyi (Waw shu-yow fahn-ee)

Please write it down
Qing xie xia lai (Cheeng she-eh she-ah lie)

Please write it in Roman letters
Qing yong Pinyin xie (Cheeng young Peen-een she-eh)

Please write it in Chinese *Qing yong Zhongwen xie*
(Cheeng young Joong-wun she-eh)

Can you go with me? *Ni neng he wo yiqi qu ma?*
(Nee nuung huh waw ee-chee chuu mah?)

Where is the toilet?
Cesuo zai nali? (T'suh-swaw jzigh nah-lee?)

It's hot! *Man re du!* (Mahn ruh duu!)

It's cold! *Man leng de!* (Mahn luung duh!)

It's raining *Xia yu le* (She-ah yuu luh)

It's windy *Feng da* (Fuung dah)

At the Restaurant

What time is dinner?
Wancan shi jidian. (Wahn t'aahn ahr joo doo in.')

I'm hungry *Woe ele* (Waw uh-luh)

Let's go eat *Rang wo women qu chifan*
(Rahng waw waw-mun chu chuh-fahn)

Where shall we eat?
Women qu nali chi? (Waw-mun chuu nah-lee chuh?)

I have a reservation *Wo yuding le fangjian*
(Waw yuu-deeng luh fahng-jee-in)

I like Chinese food
Zhong can xihuan (Joong t'sahn she-hwahn)

We would like to eat Chinese food
Women xiang chi Zhongcan (Waw-mun she-ahng chuh Johng-tsan)

We would like to eat Western food
Women xiang chi Xican (Waw-mun she-ahng chuh She-tsan)

Do you have a menu in English?
You Yingwen caidan ma? (Yoe Eeeng-wren t'sai-dahn mah?)

Just a little, please
Jiu yidianr dianr (Jeo ee-dee-in-urr dee-in-urr)

That's enough *Na xie goule* (Nah she-eh go-luh)

That's too much *Na xie tai duo-le* (Nah she-eh tie dwaw-luh)

That is/was delicious! *Haochi!* (How-chuh!)

Thank you for the delicious meal
Xiexie fan tai xiong (Shay-shay fahn tie shee-ong)

Let's go get a drink
Women qu he jiu (Waw-mun chu huh jeo)

What do you want to drink? *Ni xiang he shenme?*
(Nee shee-ahng huh shuun-muh?)

I can't drink very much *Wo bu neng he tai duo*
(Waw buu nuung huh tie dwaw)

At the Office

I would like to see Mr. Li *Wo xiang kankan Li Xiansheng*
(Waw she-ahng kahn-kahn Lee She-in-shuung)

May I speak to Mr. Wang?
Wo keyi he Wang Xiansheng shuorhua ma? (Waw kuh-ee huh Wahng
Shee-in-shuung shwaw-urr-hwah mah?)

I am waiting for Mr. Li *Wo zai deng Li Xiansheng*
(Waw zigh duung Lee Shee-in-shuung)

What time does the meeting start?
Huiyi jidian kai shi? (Hwee-ee jee-dee-in kigh shr?)

What time is the appointment?
Yuehui shi jidian? (Yu-eh-hwee shr jee-dee-in?)

At the Hotel

Are there any messages for me?
Zheli you wo-de liuyan ma?
(Juh-lee yoh waw-duhleo-yahn mah?)

Where is your business service center?
Nali shi shangwu fuwu zhongxin?
(Nah-lee shr shahng-wuu fuu-wuu joong-sheen?)

On the Road

I want to go to the railroad station
Wo yao qu huoche zhan (Waw yah-oh chuu hwa-chuh jahn)

Where is the ticket office? _Nali shi shou piao chu?_
(Nah-lee shr show pee-ow chuu?)

I want to go to the airport _Wo yao qu feiji chang_
(Waw yah-oh chuu fay-jee chahng)

How long does it take to get to the airport?
Dao jichang yao duoshao shijian?
(Dow jee-chahng yow dwaw-shou shr-jee-in?)

Please call me a taxi
Qing gei wo jiao che (Cheeng gay waw jee-ow chuh)

The airport, please
Qing qu jichang (Cheeng chu jee-chahng)

Please take me to this address
Quing dai wo dao zheige dizhi
(Cheeng die waw dow jay-guh dee-jr)

Please go to Tiananmen Square
Qing qu Tiananmen Guang Cheng
(Cheeng chu Tee-in Ahn-mun Gwahng Chuung)

Can you wait for me?
Ni neng deng wo ma? (Nee nuung duung waw mah?)

Please wait just a moment
Qing deng yi xia (Cheeng duung ee she-ah)

How much do I owe you?
Wo gai fu ni duoshao? (Waw guy fuu nee doe-sha-oh?)

I prefer to walk
Wo xi huan zuo lu (Waw she hwahn zwaw luu)

Is it too far to walk?
Zuo lu qu tai yuan-le? (Zwaw luu chuu tie wyen-luh?)

What time are we leaving?
Women shenme shijina zou?
(Waw-mun shuun-muh shr-jee-in zoe?)

Technology and Communications

Let me see your cell phone for a second
Rang wo kankan ni de shou ji
(Rahng waw kahn-kahn nee duh show jee)

Let's go to a computer store
Zanmen qu diannao shangdian ba
(Zahn-men chuu dee-in-now shahng-dee-in bah)

May I use your computer? *Wo keyi yong jisuanji ma?*
(Waw kuh-ee young jee-suu-ahn-jee mah?)

I found you on Google!
Wo zai gougou sousuoyinqing shang chadao ni le! (Waw zigh go-go soe-swaw-een-cheeng shahng chah-dow nee luh!)

Show me your homepage *Rang wo kankan nide wangye*
(Rahng waw kahn-kahn nee-duh wahng-yeh)

I want to log on to the Internet
Wo xiang zai wang shang denglu
(Waw she-ahng dzye wahng shahng duung-luu)

You must log on first
Ni bi xu xian denglu (Nee bee shu she-ahn duung-luu) OR *Shou xian ni bi xu denglu*
(Show she-in nee bee shuu dung-luu)

My computer has been infected by a worm (virus)
Wo-de diannao ganran le yizhong bingdu
(Waw-duh dee-in-now gahn-rahn luh ee-joong beeng-duu)

Where is the post office?
Youju zai nali? (Yoe-juu zigh nah-lee)

Money

Where can I exchange money? *Nali keyi duihuan qian?*
(Nah-lee kuh-ee dwee-hwahn chee-in?)

Where is the closest ATM?
Li zheli zuijin de zidong tikuanji zainaer? (Lee juh-lee zway-jeen duh dzu-doong tee-kwahn-jee zigh-nar?)

How much is that in U.S. dollars?
Zhe zhi duoshao Mei yuan?
(Juh jr dwaw-sha-oh May ywen?)

Helpful Vocabulary

abroad *guowai* (gwaw-wigh)

address *dizhi* (dee-jr)

advisor *guwen* (guu-wun)

airline *hangkong gongsi* (hahng-koong goong-suh)

flight *hangban* (hahng-bahn)

flight number *hangban haoma* (hahng-bahn how-mah)

ambassador *dashi* (dah-shr)

amount, sum, total *jin e* (jeen uh)

appointment *yuehui* (yu-eh-whee)

appraise *gujia* (guu-jah)

arbiter *zhongedizhe* (johng-eh-dzuh)

arbitration *zhongedi* (john-eh-dee)

assistant manager *shuli jingli* (shuu-lee jeeng-lee)

baggage *xingli* (sheeng-lee)

bank *yinhang* (eeen-hang)

bankrupt *pochan* (poe-chahn)

banquet *yanhui* (yahn-whee)

bar (drinking) *jiuba* (jeo-bah)

bargain (to) *taojia* (tough-jah)

barter *yihuo yihuo* (ee-hoe ee-hoe)

board of directors *dongshi hui* (doong-she hwee)

bookkeeper *kuaiji* (kwie-jee)

boyfriend *nan pengyou* (nahn puung-yoe)

bribery *huilu* (whee-luu)

budget *yusuan* (yuu-swahn)

business *shangye* (shahng-yeh)

business hours *yingye shijian* (eeng-eh she-jee-inn)

businessperson *shangren* (shahng-wren)

buy *mai* (my)

cash *xiankuan* (she-inn kwan)

cell phone *shou ji* (show jee)

China *Zhongguo* (Joong-gwaw)

Chinese (people) *Zhongren* (Joong-wren)

Chinese character/ideogram *hanzi* (hahn-dzu)

cocktail party *jiweijiu hui* (jee-way-jeo whee)

coffee *kafei* (kah-fay)

coffee shop *kafei dian* (kah-fay dee-in)

company/corporation *gongsi* (goong-suh)

competition *jingzheng* (jeeng-juung)

computer *diannao* (dee-in-now)

conference *huiyi* (whee-ee)

conference room *huiyi shi* (whee-ee shr)

consulate *lingshiguan* (leeng-shr-gwahn)

consulting company *zixun gongsi* (jee-shuun goong-suh)

corruption *fubai* (fuu-by)

cost *chengben* (chuung-ben)

credit card *xinyong ka* (sheen-yoong kah)

culture *wenhua* (wun-hwah)

customs *haiguan* (hi-gwahn)

customs tariff *guanshui shuize* (gwahn-shwee shway-zuh)

daily paper *ri bao* (re bow)

department (of company/organization) *bu* (buu)

department store *baihuo dian* (buy-hwaw dee-in)

deposit (money) *yajin* (yah-jeen)

director *dongshi* (doogn-shuh)

discount *zhekou* (juh-koe)

distributor *xiaoshou zhongxin* (she-ow-show joohng-sheen)

doctor *yisheng* (ee-shuung)

dollar(s) *meiyuan* (may-ywen)

domestic call *guonei dianhua* (gway-nay dee-in-hwah)

driver's license *jiashi zhishao* (jee-ah-shr jr-shou)

drugstore *yaodian* (yow-dee-in)

drunk, tipsy *zui* (zway)

duty free *mianshui* (me-inn shwee)

economy *jingli* (jeeng-lee)

electrical goods *dianqi pin* (dee-in-chee peen)

embassy *dashiguan* (dah-shr-gwahn)

employee *gongzuorenyuan* (goong-zwaw-wren-ywen)

engineer *gongchengshi* (goong-chuung-shr)

enterprise *qiye* (chee-yeh)

entry visa *rujing qianzheng* (ruu-jeeng chee-in-juung)

evening dress *wan lifu* (wahn lee-fuu)

exchange rate *duihuan tu* (dwee-hwahn-tuu)

exhibition *zhanlanhui* (jahn-lahn-hway)

exhibition hall *zhanlan guan* (jahn-lahn gwahn)

expenses *feiyong* (fay-yoong)

export *chukou* (chuu-koe)

export duty *chukuo shui* (chuu-koe shway)

export license *chukou xuke zheng* (chuu-koe shu-kuh-juung)

factory *gongchang* (goong-chahng)

fashion *shimao* (shr-mou)

foreign exchange *waihui* (wie-hwee)

free trade zone *ziyou maoyiqu* (dzu-yoe mou-ee-chu)

gasoline *qiyou* (chee-yoe)

gasoline station *jiayou zhan* (jow-yoe-jahn)

general manager *zongjingli* (joong-jeeng-lee)

gift *liwu* (lee-wuu)

girlfriend *nu pengyou* (nuu puung-yoe)

government *zhengfu* (juung-fuu)

Great Wall of China *Chang Cheng* (Chahng Chuung)

green tea *lu cha* (luu chah)

guide *daoyou* (dow-yoe)

hello! *wei!* (way!)

holiday *jiaqi* (jah-chee)

host, owner *zhuren* (juu-wren)

hotel *luguan* (luu-gwahn)

illegal *buhefa-de* (buu-huh-fah-duh)

import *finkou* (feen-koe)/*jinkou* (jeen-koe)

import duty *jinkou shui* (jeen-koe shwee)

import license *jinkou xukezheng* (jeen-koe shu-kuh-jung)

income *shouru* (show-ruu)

income tax *suode shui* (swaw-duh shwee)

information desk *wenxunchu* (wun-shwun-chuu)
in-house phone *nei-xian dianhua* (nay she-in dee-in-hwah)
insurance *baoxian* (bow-she-inn)
international *guoji* (gwaw-jee)
international call *guowai dianhua* (gwaw-wie dee-in-hwah)
international law *guoji fa* (gwoh-jee fah)
interpreter *fanyi* (fahn-ee)
investment *touzi* (toe-dzu)
joint venture *hezi qiye* (huh-jee chee-yeh)
journalist *jizhe* (jee-dzeh)
judge (person) *faguan* (fah-gwahn)
justice *gongzheng* (goong-juung)
kilogram *gongjin* (goong-jeen)
kilometer *gongli* (goong-lee)
lawsuit *susong* (suu-soong)
lawyer *lushi* (luu-shuh)
license *xuke zheng* (shu-kuh juung)
loan *daikuan* (die-kwahn)
lobby *qianting* (chee-in-teeng)
local call *dangdi dianhua* (dahng-dee dee-in-hwah)
long-distance call *changtu dianhua* (chahng-tuu dee-in-hwah)
loss *kui sun* (kwee suun)
mahjong *majiang* (mah-jee-ahng)
maitre d' *zongguan* (zoong-gwahn)
manager *jingli* (jeeng-lee)
management *guanli* (gwahn-lee)
market *shichang* (shr-chahng)
marketing *shichang yingxiao* (shuh-chahng eeng-she-ow)
market price *shichang jiage* (shuh-chahng-jah-guh)
mechanic *jigong* (jee-goong)
meeting *hui* (whee)
military *junshi* (Juun-shr)
mobile phone *shou ji* (show jee)
musician *yinyue jia* (een-yuu-eh jee-ah)
nation *guo* (gwaw)
national defense *guofang* (gwaw-fahng)

national flag *guoqi* (gwaw-chee)

nationality *minzu* (meen-zoo)

necktie *lingdai* (leeng-die)

newspaper *baozhi* (bow-jr)

New Year *Xin Nian Yuandan* (Sheen Nee-in Ywen-dahn)

New Year's Eve *Chu Xi* (Chuu She)

nightclub *ye zonghui* (yeh joong-whee)

occupation *zhiye* (jr-yeh)

office hours *bangong shijian* (bahn-goon shr-jee-in)

office worker *zhi yuan* (jr ywen)

official *guan* (gwahn)

official business *gong wu* (goong wuu)

overseas *guowai* (gwaw-wie)

overseas Chinese *Hua Qiao* (Hwah Chee-ow)

ownership *yongyouquan* (young-yoe-chwahn)

partner *hehuo ren* (heh-hoe wren)

passport *huzhao* (huu-jow)

patent *zhuanli* (juu-ahn-lee)

payment *fu kuan* (fuu kwahn)

petroleum *shiyou* (shr-yoe)

phone (call) *dianhua* (dee-in-hwah)

police *jingcha* (jeeng-chah)

police station *gongganju* (goong-gahn-juu)

politics *zhengzhi* (juung-jr)

pollution *wuran* (wuu-rahn)

population *renkou* (wren-koe)

post office *you ju* (yoe-juu)

premier *zongli* (zoong-lee)

price *jiage* (jah-guh)

product *chanpin* (chahn-peen)

professional *zhuanye-de* (jwahn-yeh-duh)

professor *jiaoshou* (jee-ow-shohh)

profit *lirun* (lee-ruun)

property *caichan* (t'sie-chahn)

province *sheng* (shuung)

public relations *gonggong guanxi* (goong-goong-gwahn-she) public telephone *gongyong dianhua* (goong-yoong-dee-in-hwah)

Public Security Bureau *Gong Anju* (Goong Ahn-juu)

purchasing agent *daiyou ren* (die-yoe wren)

quality *zhiliang* (jr-lee-ahng)

quantity *shuliang* (shuu-lee-ahng)

quota *ding-e* (deeng-uh)

railway station *huochezhan* (hwaw-chuh-jahn)

receipt *shouju* (show-juu)

reception, party *zhaodaihui* (jow-die-hwee)

reception desk *fuwutai* (fuu-wuu-tie)

receptionist *jiedaiyuan* (jee-eh-die-ywen)

refund *tuikuan* (tway-kwahn)

region *diqu* (dee-chuu)

rent, hire *zu* (zoo)

reservations *yuding* (yuu-deeng)

restaurant *fanguan* (fahn-gwahn)

retail *lingshou* (leeng-show)

room number *fangjian haoma* (fahng-jee-inn how-mah)

sale *xiaoshou* (she-ow-show)

sales manager *xiaoshou jingli* (shee-ow-show jeeng-lee)

sales person *shouhuoyuan* (show-hoe-yuu-inn)

sales tax *yingye shui* (eeng-yeh shwee)

school *xuéxiáo* (shway-she-ah-ow)

schoolmate *tongxue* (toong-shu-eh)

scientist *kexuejia* (kuh-shuu-eh-jah)

security *zheng quan* (juung chwahn)

security guard *anquan renyuan* (ahn-chwahn wren-ywen)

sell *shoumai* (show-my)

selling price *mai jia* (my-jee-ah)

seminar *yantaohui* (yahn-tou-whee)

service *fuwu* (fuu-wuu)

service attendant *fuwu yuan* (fuu-wuu ywen)

service desk *fuwu tai* (fuu-wuu tie)

service fee *fuwu fei* (fuu-wuu fay)

shake hands *wo shou* (waw show)

shipment *zhuangyun* (jwahng-ywun)

silk road *Sichou Zhi Lu* (Suh-choe Jr Luu)

store *shangdian* (shahng-dee-inn)

student *xuesheng* (shway-shuung)

subway *ditie* (de-tee-eh)

subway station *ditie chezhan* (dee-tee-eh chuh-jahn)

tax *shui* (shwee)

tax free *mian shui* (me-in shwee)

technology *jishu gongyi* (jee-shuu goong-ee)

technology transfer *jishu zhuanrang* (jee-shuu jwahn-rahng)

telephone *dianhua* (dee-inn-hwah)

telephone number *dianhua haoma* (dee-in-hwah how-mah)

telephone directory *dianhua bu* (dee-in-hwah buu)

teacher *laoshi* (lough-shrr)

Tibet *Xizang* (She-zahng)

trade, commerce *maoyi* (mow-ee)

trade fair *jiaoyi hui* (jee-ow hwee)

trademark *shang biao* (shahng bee-ow)

translate, translator *fanyi* (fahn-ee)

transportation *yunshu* (ywun-shuu)

transportation charges *yunshu feiyong* (ywun-shuu fay-yoong)

travel, trip *luxing* (luu-sheeng)

travel agent *luxing she* (luu-sheeng shuh)

United States *Meiguo* (May-Gwaw)

university *dáxué* (dahh-shway)

visa *qianzheng* (chee-in-juung)

wages, salary: *gongzi* (goong-zuu)

Western food *Xican* (She-t'sahn)

Western toilet *zuoshi cesuo* (zwaw-shr tsuh-swaw)

wholesale *pifa* (pee-fah)

wholly owned foreign company *waishang duzi qiye* (why-shang doo-zuh chee-yeh)

photocopier *fuyin* (fuu-een)

Yellow River *Huang He* (Hwahng Huh)

zero *ling* (leeng)

Glossary of Terms Related to Digital Communications

app *yingyong chengxu* (eeng-yong chung-shoo)
blog *boke* (boh-ku)
blog post *boke wenzhang* (boh-ku wen-jahng)
cell phone *shouji* (shoh-jee)
censorship *shencha* (shen-chah)
cloud computing *yun jisuang* (yoon jee-su-ahn)
computer *dian nao* (dee-ahn nah-oh)
computer server *jisuanji fuwuqi* (jee-su-ahn-ji foo-woo-chee)
computer network *dian nao wanglu* (dee-ahn nah-oh wang-loo)
cybersecurity *wangluo anquan* (wang-loo-ah ahn-choo-ahn)
cybersecurity laws *wangluo anquan de falu* (wang-loo-ah ahn-choo-ahn duh fah-loo)
digital communications *shuji tongxin* (shoo-jee tohng-sheen)
digital data *shuji shuju* (shoo-jee shoo-joo)
download *xiazai* (shee-ah zah-ee)
e-commerce *dianzi shangwu* (dee-ahn-zuh shahng-woo)
e-company *dianzi gongsi* (dee-ahn zuh gohng-soo)
e-store *wang dian* (wang dee-ahn)
email *dianzi youjian* (dee-ahn-zuh yoh-jee-ahn)
encryption code *jiami diama* (jee-ah-mee die-mah)
firewall *fanghuoqiang* (fang wha chee-ahng)
follower *zhuisui zhe* (joo-ee soo-ee ju)
Golden Shield Project *jindun gongcheng* (jeen-doon gong-chung)
Great Firewall of China *fanghuo changcheng* (fang-wha chang-chung) (an informal name for the Golden Shield Project)
human flesh search engines *renrou sousuo* (ren-roh soh-suah)
Internet *hulianwang* (hoo-lee-ahn-wang)
intranet *neibu wang* (nay-boo wang)
laptop *bijiben dian nao* (bee-jee-bun dee-ahn nah-oh)
Internet bar/Internet cafe *wangba* (wang-bah)

Internet provider *hulianwang fuwu tigong shang* (hoo-lee-ahn-wang foo-woo tee-gong shahng)

microblog *weixing boke* (way-sheeng boh-ku) or *weibo* (way-boh)

mobile Internet *yidong hulianwang* (ee-dong hoo-lee-ahn-wang)

netizen *wangyou* (wang-yoh)

online friend *wangyou* (wang-yoh)

online marketing *zai xian ying xiao* (zie shee-ahn eeng she-ah-oh)

password *mima* (mee-mah)

pirated media *daoban meiti* (dah-oh-bahn may-tee)

real name policy *shiming zhengce* (shee-meeng jung-tsuh)

register *zhuce* (joo-tsuh)

search *souxun* (soh-shoon)

search engine *sousuo yinqing* (soh-suah een-cheeng)

sign in *denglu* (dung-loo)

sign out *dengchu* (dung-choo)

social media *shejiao meiti* (shu-jee-ah-oh may-tee)

social network *she jiao wang luo* (shu jee-ah-oh wang lu-ah)

tablet computer *pingban dian nao* (peeng-bahn dee-ahn nah-oh)

text message *duanxin* (doo-ahn sheen)

thumb drive/U-disk *muzhi qudongqi* (moo-jee choo-dong-chee) or U-*pan* (yoo-pahn)

upload *shangzai* (shahn-zah-ee)

VPN *xuni zhuanyong wang* (shoo-nee joo-ahn-yong wang) or VPN

web browser *wangye liulan qi* (wang-yuh leo-lahn chee)

website *wangzhan* (wang-jahn)

webpage *wangye* (wang-yuh)

web portal *menhu wangzhan* (mun-hoo wang-jahn)

Using email in China

email address 电子邮件地址 *dianzi youjian dizhi* (dee-ahn-zu yoh-jee-ahn dee-ju)

sign/log in 登录 *denglu* (dung-loo)

inbox 收件箱 *shoujianxiang* (shoh-jee-ahn-shee-ahng)

sent messages/outbox 发送的邮件 *fasong de youjian* (fah-song duh yoh-jee-ahn) or 发件箱 *fajianxiang* (fa-jee-ahn-shee-ahng)

drafts 草稿 *caogao* (tsah-oh gah-oh)

spam 垃圾邮件 *lese youjian* (luh-suh yoh-jee-ahn) or *laji youjian* (lah-ji yoh-jee-ahn)

deleted messages 已删除邮件 *yi shanchu youjian* (ee shahn-choo yoh-jee-ahn)

compose/write an email 写邮件 *xie youjian* (shee-eh yoh-jee-ahn)

addressee 收件人 *shou jianren* (shoh jee-ahn-ren)

subject 主题 *zhuti* (joo-tee)

cc 抄送 *chao song* (chah-oh song)

bcc 密送 *mi song* (mee song)

reply 回复 *huifu* (whey-foo)

reply all 全部回复 *quanbu huifu* (choo-ahn-boo whey-foo)

forward 转发 *zhuanfa* (joo-ahn fah)

email attachment 电子邮件附件 *dian youjian fujian* (dee-ahn-zu yoh-jee-ahn foo-jee-ahn)

print 打印 *dayin* (dah-een)

send 发送 *fa song* (fah song)

Phrases for use in email

Dear (name and title)
尊敬的 (name and title)
zunjing de (zoon-jeeng duh)

To: (name and title)
致: (name and title)
zhi (jih)

We are writing to you regarding ...
我们就 ... 一事给您写信。
women jiu ... yishi gei nin xie xin.
(woh-mun jeo ... ee-shuh gay nee shee-ay sheen)

With reference to your company ...
鉴于贵公司 ...
jianyu gui gongsi ...
(jee-an-yoo goo-ee gong-su)

I am writing to inquire for information about ...
我写信，想询问关于 ... 的信息。
wo xie xin, xiang xunwen guanyu ... de xinxi.
(woh shee-ay sheen, shee-ahng shoon-wun goo-ahn-yoo ... duh sheen-shee)

Please let us know about your ...
请先告知贵方 ...
qing xian gaozhi gui fang ...
(cheeng shee-ahn gah-oh-juh goo-ee fang)

We would be grateful if ...
如果您能 ...，我们将不胜感激。
ruguo nin neng ..., women jiang bu sheng ganji.
(roo-goh neen nung ..., woh-mun jee-ahng boo shung gahn-jee)

Please see the attachment.
请参阅该附件。
qing canyue gai fujian.
(cheeng tsahn-yoo-eh gah-ee foo-jee-an)

Thank you for your assistance.
非常感谢您的协助.
feichang ganxie nin de xiezhu.
(fay-chang gahn-shee-ay neen duh shee-ay-joo)

Thank you in advance.
提前谢谢您。
tiqian xiexie nin.
(tee-chee-ahn shay-shay neen)

I'm looking forward to your early reply.
盼早日回复!
pan zaori huifu.
(pahn zah-oh-ree hoo-ee-foo)

Yours sincerely,

<u>(your name)</u>
此致
敬礼

<u>(your name)</u>
cizhi
jingli
(tsuh-juh
jeeng-lee)

Wishing you well!

(your name)
此祝
"安好!"

(your name)
cizhu
anhao!
(tsuh-joo
ahn-hah-oh)

Regards, (literally, "Good luck!")

(your name)
祝好
(your name)
zhu hao
(joo-hah-oh)

Index

A

Agricultural technology, 18
Alcohol, 77–78, 155–156
Apologies, 31, 70–71
Authority levels, 149

B

Back door connections, 58–59, 109
Ba (eight), 46
Baijiu, 78
Bamboo gifts, 86
Banquets, 79–82, 153–154
Birthdays, 83
Bo Xilia, 23–24
Body language and hand gestures,
    68–69
Bowing and shaking hands, 68
Budan xin (sincerity plus
    understanding), 101–102
Bu shi (not true), 71
Business. See also Negotiating;
    Personal etiquette
  back door connections, 58, 109
  collective well-being and, 118
  connections (*guanxi*), 45, 52,
      57–58, 107–108, 110, 150
  connections vs. competence,
      57–58
  corporate titles, 165
  cultural influences on, 111–124
  culture barrier, 100
  dealing with 56 Chinas, 95–96
  dossier factor, 103–104
  general guidelines, 75–86
  government big brother and, 96–99
  group orientation vs.
      individualism, 119–122
  as guerilla warfare, 111–112
  Hong Kong and, 59–61
  information black hole, 109
  intellectual piracy, 124
  introductions, 108, 139
    Personal vs. Group
      Accountability, 121, 122
  nature of relationships, 15
  not rotating managers, 110
  office phrases, 170–171, 183–184
  production vs. consumption,
      117–118
  professional education, 102–103
  secrecy syndrome, 116–117
  self-sufficiency emphasis, 121
  senior/junior factor, 112–113
  Shanghai and, 31–32, 61–62
  social etiquette, 104–106
  two-dimensional vs. three-
      dimensional thinking, 117
  using back door connections, 109
  women in, 104
  yes and *no*, 71, 123
Business cards, 139–140
Business entertainment, 152–157.
  See also Meals and celebrations
  alcohol and, 155–156
  answering personal questions, 156
  banquets, 153–155
  general guidelines and overview,
      151–153
  gift-giving and, 83–86, 156–157
  hosting banquets, 154–155
  hosting Chinese delegations,
      158–161
  paying bills, 161
  toasting, 153, 155
Bu yao keqi (you are welcome), 65

C

Capitalism, rise of, 28, 112

Celebrations. *See* Meals and
celebrations
Changing role of foreigners in the
workplace, 90–95
Charm schools, 32
Chengyu, 16
Children
education laws, 50
little emperors, 28–29
names of, 67–68
one-per-couple policy, 28–29
Chinese businesspeople, old versus
new generation of, 113–116
Chopsticks, 75–77
Civilization
Chinese, eclipse of, 18–19
Chinese impact on, 13–18
Collective well-being, 56–57,
118–119
Comfort zone (between people),
68–69
Communism. *See also* Mao Zedung
dating/marriage and, 73–74
gift-giving ban, 83–84, 156–157
government big brother and,
96–99
Mandarin as primary language
and, 9–10
names of children and, 67–68
personal favors and, 106–108
religion and, 69–70
sensitive discussion topic, 69–70
Shanghai and, 62
takeover of, 18–19, 60–61
women in business world and,
29–30, 104, 113
women's rights and, 50 51
Communist Party, growth of, 23
Confucius
Cultural Revolution and, 20,
112–113
hierarchy-based system today,
112–113
laws and philosophy, 13–15, 42,
54–55, 96–97, 112–113
non-standard nature of laws, 42–43

relevance of laws, 13–14, 54–55
ritualism of etiquette rules and,
13–15
secrecy of laws and, 116–117
silence in negotiating and,
148–149
on virtues of jade, 86
Connections (*guanxi*), 52, 57–59,
84–85, 107–110, 150
Consonants, 10
Contracts, 99, 123, 133–134, 150
Cultural influences on etiquette,
42–62. *See also* Confucius
business-related, 111–124
connections vs. competence, 57–58
dragon culture, 44–45
face, 51–53, 105–108, 127–128,
154–155, 160–161
feng shui, 46–47
Hong Kong and, 59–62
law vs. reality, 54–55
lucky numbers, 46–47
overview, 42–43
perspective on foreigners, 27,
100–101
public vs. private rights, 56–57
rights and roles of women, 50–51
Shanghai and, 61–62
using back door connections,
53–54, 109–110
what/how vs. why/because, 54
yin-yang principle, 22–23
Cultural Revolution
description and effects of, 14–16,
120
enduring legacy of, 20, 31
generations born after, 27
religion and, 56, 69–70
senior/junior factor and, 112–113,
116
Culture
Chinese word for, 7
country name and, 7
defined, 7
Mao Zedung impact on values,
19–20, 31, 70, 73–74

power of, 13–15
Culture barrier, 54, 100–102, 129–130

D

Dai ji juan, 144
Dang'an (personal dossier), 103–110, 129
Dating and marriage, 73–74. *See also* Marriage
Deng Xiaoping, 21–25, 124
Discussion topics, 69–70
Diu-mian-zi (embarrassing acts), 53–54
Domestic violence, 50
Dossier factor, 103–110, 129
Dragon culture, 44–45

E

Education, 50, 102–103
Er (two), 46
Etiquette. *See also* Personal etiquette
Chinese perspective on, 7–9
Chinese word for, 7
enforcement of, 7–8, 10
female guru, 29–30
Mao Zedung regime and, 8–9
in new global age, 30–32
one-child system impacting, 28–29
origins of, 13–15. *See also* Confucius
Seven Don'ts, 32
training in, 8
Expressions. *See* Vocabulary and expressions

F

Face, role of, 51–54, 105–108, 127–128, 147–149, 154–155, 160–161
Fa (making fortune), 46
Family names, using, 65–67
Family relationships, 119, 164–165
Feng shui (wind and water), 45–46
Folk tales and proverbs, 16–17
Foreign experts, 91–95
Foreigners, perspective on, 47–49

G

Ganbei (bottoms up), 152, 155–156
Gei-mian-zi (showing respect/complimenting), 52–53
Gestures and body language, 68–69
Gift-giving, 73–74, 82–86, 157
Go-betweens, 106, 149–150
Government and politics. *See also* Communism
big-brother government, 96–99
government titles, 165
professional education and, 94
Great Firewall of China, 38–39
Greetings, 65–67, 139, 164, 166–167
Group orientation and the Chinese education system, 119–120
Group orientation vs. individualism, 119–121
Guanxi (connections), 57–59, 84, 94, 107–110, 114, 150, 168, 178

H

Hand gestures and body language, 68–69
Health contributions, of China, 18, 45
Hen gaoxing renshi ni (I'm pleased to meet you), 140, 167
Home visits, 73
Hong Kong, 9, 21, 59–62, 90, 93
Honorable guest factor, 79
Hosting Chinese delegations, 158–159
Hotel phrases, 170–171
Hou men (back door) connections, 58, 109
Hui bao (mutual reciprocity), 107
Hukou, 22

I

Information black hole, 109
Intellectual piracy, 124
Internet, 8, 28, 33, 35, 37–40, 94, 173, 181–185
Internet in China, 33–41
Internet censorship, 34, 36–39
Interpreters, 80, 135–136, 155

Intimate behavior in public, 74
Introductions, 90, 108, 139, 159
Inventions, 17–18

J

Jack Ma, 33–34, 115
Jade, 86
Jiang-mian-zi (respect, increasing face), 53

K

Kan, Yue-Sae, 29–30
Keqi (polite, well mannered), 65, 168

L

Language (Chinese). *See also* Vocabulary and expressions
    consonants, 10
    family of languages comprising, 9
    Mandarin as primary, 9
    pronunciation note, 9–10
    vowels, 10
Lao Tzu, 15–16, 20, 54, 146
Law vs. reality, 54–55
Lei Feng, 17
Li (etiquette), 7
Little emperors, 28–29
Liu-mian-zi (good reputation), 52
Liu (six), 46
Lucky numbers, 46–47

M

Mandarin language, 9–10, 19, 60, 141, 164. *See also* Vocabulary and expressions
Moutai (drink), 78, 153
Mao Zedung
    communist regime of, 8–9, 19
    Cultural Revolution legacy, 19
    death of, 21
    impact on cultural values, 8, 19, 43, 68–69, 73, 104
Ma, Pony, 33
Marriage
    arranged, 73–74
    dating and, 30, 73–74

historic perspective, 73–74
    intimate behavior in public, 74
    law giving women property/ inheritance rights, 50
    today, 74
    Western-style, 68, 74
    women keeping family name after, 66
Maybe, 72
Meals and celebrations, 75–86. *See also* Business entertainment
    alcohol and, 77–78, 152–153, 155–156
    banquets, 153–154, 156
    birthdays, 83
    chopsticks and, 75–77
    general guidelines, 75–86
    gift-giving and, 83–86, 156–157, 161
    honorable guest factor, 79
    restaurant phrases, 169–170
    sitting in right place, 81–88
    tea and, 78–79, 160, 176
    tipping, 79–80
    wedding banquets, 82
Meiyǒu (no), 71
Mianzi (face or personal honor), 51–54, 100–107, 127
Modesty, 72–73
Money, 172

N

Nali? Nali? (Where? Where?), 72–73, 169, 171–172
Name, of China (in Chinese), 7
Names
    common, 66
    family, using, 65–66
    getting to know each other, 169–170
    given, using, 67–68
    nicknames, 68
Negotiating, 131–151
    addressing senior person, 134
    asking right questions, 144
    attention to small details, 137, 154

authority levels and, 141–149
business cards and, 139
competitors as bogeymen in, 148
compromising effectively,
    148–149
confirming mutual
    understanding, 143
contracts and, 99, 123, 150
curbing enthusiasm during, 142
dressing for, 137–138
fact/truth vs. how things are
    done, 129–130
fielding first team, 135
formality of, 139–141
friendship factor, 128–129
go-betweens in, 149–150
greetings and, 68, 139–141
"hit-run" tactic, 145
humor caution, 137
if they leave room, 146–147
importance of technology, 132
interpreters for, 135–136
intimidation and anger tactics,
    143, 147
leaving lawyers out, 136
never forget, never forgive, 131–132
note taking and, 143
passive face ploy, 145
persistence in, 150–151
posture and, 142
power of face, 127–128
presentation length, 143
process overview, 127, 129–130,
    139–141
senior people and, 134, 141–142
silence in, 146
social status and, 133–134
striking like a snake, 144
summarizing meeting, 143
thinking holistically, 129
ultimatum taboo, 132
what to expect, 139–151
withholding information and, 145
New China
    etiquette in global age, 30–32
    little emperors and, 28–29

overview, 26–28
Yue-Sai Kan and, 29–30
No and *yes*, 71–72, 123
Numbers, lucky, 46–47

O

One-Child Policy, 28–29

P

Passive face ploy, 145
Personal etiquette, 65–74
    apologies, 70–71
    comfort zone between people,
        68–69
    dating and marriage, 73–74
    hand gestures and body language,
        68–69
    home visits, 73
    intimate behavior in public, 74
    modesty, 72–73
    overview, 65
    sensitive discussion topics, 69–70
    shaking hands and bowing, 68
    using family names, 65–66
    using given names, 67–68
    yes and *no*, 71–72
Policy of Reform and Opening Up,
    21
Pollution, 31
Pony Ma, 33
Private vs. public rights, 56–57
Production vs. consumption,
    117–118
Pronunciation note, 9–10
Public displays of affection, 74
Public vs. private rights, 56–57

Q

Qi (cosmic energy), 45

R

Reality vs. law, 54–55
Religion, 69–70
Renrou sousuo (human flesh search
    engines), 35
Respect (face), 51–54
Rights, public vs. private, 56–57

Rule of law, 22–24

S

Secrecy syndrome, 116–117
Self-sufficiency emphasis, 121
Senior/junior factor, 112–113
Sentences. *See* Vocabulary and
    expressions
Seven Don'ts, 31–32
Shaking hands and bowing, 68
Shanghai, 61–62
Shenzhen, 21
Si (four), 46
Social etiquette, in business world,
    104–106. *See also* Meals and
    celebrations; Personal etiquette
Social status, 133–134

T

Tea, 78–79
Tiananmen Square protests, 21
Tipping, 79–80
Titles, 65–66, 164–165
Toasting, 80–82, 153, 155
Travel phrases, 171
Two-dimensional vs. three-
    dimensional thinking, 117

U

Urbanization, 22

V

Vocabulary and expressions,
    164–185
    alphabetic vocabulary list, 174–180
    conversation phrases, 168–169
    corporate titles, 165
    everyday expressions, 166
    family relationships, 164–165
    getting to know each other,
        167–168
    government titles, 165
    hotel phrases, 170–171
    money, 172
    office phrases, 172
    personal titles, 164
    pronunciation note, 9–10
    restaurant phrases, 169–170
    technology and communications,
        172–173
    traveling, 171–172
    useful sentences, 168–173
    Vowels, 10
Vocabulary and phrases used in
    email, 182–185
Vocabulary related to digital
    communications, 181–182

W

Wenhua, 7
Westerners, Chinese perspective
    on, 47–49
Westerners in the Chinese Digital
    World, 39–41
What/how vs. why/because, 54
Women
    in business world, 104
    domestic violence and, 50
    education and, 50
    equality and Communist Party,
        50
    keeping family name after
        marriage, 66
    rights and roles, 50–51
    today, 50–51
Wumao dang (50-cent army), 35–36

X

Xi Jinping, 24

Y

Yes and *no*, 71–72, 123
Yin-yang principle, 43–44
Yue-Sai Kan, 29–30
Yŏu (yes), 71

Z

Zhong Hua, 7
Zhongjian ren (go-betweens),
    149–150

ABOUT TUTTLE
"Books to Span the East and West"

Our core mission at Tuttle Publishing is to create books which bring people together one page at a time. Tuttle was founded in 1832 in the small New England town of Rutland, Vermont (USA). Our fundamental values remain as strong today as they were then—to publish best-in-class books informing the English-speaking world about the countries and peoples of Asia. The world has become a smaller place today and Asia's economic, cultural and political influence has expanded, yet the need for meaningful dialogue and information about this diverse region has never been greater. Since 1948, Tuttle has been a leader in publishing books on the cultures, arts, cuisines, languages and literatures of Asia. Our authors and photographers have won numerous awards and Tuttle has published thousands of books on subjects ranging from martial arts to paper crafts. We welcome you to explore the wealth of information available on Asia at www.tuttlepublishing.com.

Published by Tuttle Publishing, an imprint of Periplus Editions (HK) Ltd

www.tuttlepublshing.com

Copyright © 2008 Boye Lafayette de Mente
Revisions Copyright © 2016 Periplus Editions HK. Ltd

All rights reserved. No part of this publication may be reproduced or utilized in any form or by any means, electronic or mechanical, including photocopying, recording, or by any information storage and retrieval system, without prior written permission from the publisher.

ISBN 978-0-8048-4519-9

TUTTLE PUBLISHING® is a registered trademark of Tuttle Publishing, a division of Periplus Editions (HK) Ltd.

Distributed by

North America, Latin America & Europe
Tuttle Publishing
364 Innovation Drive,
North Clarendon,
VT 05759-9436 U.S.A.
Tel: (802) 773-8930;
Fax: (802) 773-6993
info@tuttlepublishing.com;
www.tuttlepublishing.com

Asia Pacific
Berkeley Books Pte. Ltd.
61 Tai Seng Avenue
#02-12, Singapore 534167
Tel: (65) 6280-1330;
Fax: (65) 6280-6290
inquiries@periplus.com.sg
www.periplus.com

Printed in China   1606CM
20 19 18 17 16
10 9 8 7 6 5 4 3 2 1